INTRO'

Ten Introverts That Built Modern Society and
Influenced the World We Live in

(The Advantage of Being an Introvert in an
Extrovert World)

Angela Weatherby

Published by Harry Barnes

Angela Weatherby

All Rights Reserved

ISBN 978-1-7751430-8-6

Legal & Disclaimer

The information contained in this book is not designed to replace or take the place of any form of medicine or professional medical advice. The information in this book has been provided for educational and entertainment purposes only.

The information contained in this book has been compiled from sources deemed reliable, and it is accurate to the best of the Author's knowledge; however, the Author cannot guarantee its accuracy and validity and cannot be held liable for any errors or omissions. Changes are periodically made to this book. You must consult your doctor or get professional medical advice before using any of the

Table of Contents

Introduction

Thanks for taking the time to download this guide, hopefully inside you will find a range of information and details that can help you become a Better, Bigger, and Bolder person.

What is your personality trait in life? Do you like people? Do you get on easily with people? Are you socially inclined or declined? Are you reclusive, implosive or explosive? Are you risk-averse or you are a risk taker? Do you want to find a partner? What is your outlook on life? Well, whatever your answer is/are immensely betrays the stuff you are made of.

Strangely enough, many folks have tried for years to find their true personality. Some people thought they were active while their true personality was cheerful. And sometimes, a person thinks they are friendly when it turns out they are distant. Well, if you are not totally sure about your personality, do not be dismayed. After reading through this Book, you would have done absolute justice to that. You would have been in the "know"- knowing your true trait.

Chapter 1: Life Of An Introvert

A few days ago, in a parallel universe, there was an angel whom I got connected with, the angel who helped me find a hidden treasure, the treasure that I was unaware about. The treasure which was always so close to me, which was a part of my personality, which never surfaced up just like a male musk deer is unaware of the pleasant fragrance that originates from its navel area. I never expected that this little angel and the conversation with them will spark up my life forever. And it was only then when I started working on this book.

I like spending time by myself which is the way I refill my inner self; yes, I accept that I am an introvert. People who are introverted tend to be focused more on internal thoughts, feelings and moods rather than seeking out external stimulation, we can say they are inward turning.The term "introvert" describes a person who tends to turn inward mentally.

The introverts sometimes avoid large groups of people, feeling more energized by spending their time alone. It's their way to fuel up their inner self. Not all the introverts are of the same degree, not everyone knows if they are introverts or not.

This book will prove to be a revolution, it will give more power to introverts, it will motivate them to pursue what they want and to embrace themselves for who they are. It will prove to be pain reliever which will alleviate the pain that is caused from feeling inferior, less worthy or different by the treatment from the society and due to prevailing social stigma. People will start realizing that being an introvert is not a disabilitynor it's any kind of a defect or disorder,it's just a choice and a way of living life.

An introvert is a quiet person who is more interested in its own ideas and feelings rather than in spending time with other people, some people describe introverts as people who think a lot but speak very little.

Introversion and extroversion are personality dimensions which individuals differ on scale. Introverts are quiet and shy, while extroverts are loud, sociable and outgoing.

Introverts actually don't hate people as generally thought in our society; they just feel better when they aren't around them as being surrounded by people drains their energy. Mostly introverts find it really hard to have an eye contact with someone, however when they do, their heart starts to beat faster, their limbs start to shiver and some people can get anxiety attacks as well.

There is not just one way to be an introvert; rather, there are various versions of introversion; there are people who prefer smaller groups, people who imagine and think a lot, people who lack confidence, and people who don't like talking much. In fact, many introverts have combined qualities of these types, rather than demonstrating just a single type over the others.

There is a population of introverts who have a preference for socializing with smaller groups instead of larger ones, some prefer no group at all; solitude is often preferable for such people in this kind of introversion. This kind of introversion is the closest to the common man's understanding of introversion. People with such a behavior prefer to stay home with a book or working on a computer, some may prefer to stick to smaller parties with close friends, in contrast to attending large gatherings with many strangers.

Some people like to think a lot and they sometimes are too much carried away into their thinking that they lose the sense of their surroundings. People with high levels of compulsiveness of imagining don't like the idea to participate in social events. Instead, they are introspective, thoughtful, and self-reflective. They have a capability of getting lost in an internal fantasy world, and they enjoy doing that. Something to be kept in mind is there is nothing wrong with their brains instead it's just an imaginative and creative way.

A few people lack confidence and they continuously feel inferior about their capacity to deal with public; they repeatedly overthink and put themselves down in their own mindset. They have a terrible confidence level and they are worried all the time. Such people may seek out solitude because they feel awkward and painfully self-conscious when they are around other people, because they are not very confident in their own social skills. But, often, their anxiety doesn't fade when they are all alone. Such introverts are pessimistic unlike others who are always thinking positively. This kind of introversion is defined by a tendency to ponder, to turn over and over in their minds the things that might or already have gone terribly wrong. Yet another type of introversion is seen in people who need a short warm up or idling time before they can function efficiently sometimes such people seem to operate at a slightly slower pace, preferring to think before they speak or act. They also might take a while to proceed in any task or they take time before they can think about some think, first few seconds their mind is blank. Like it takes our muscles a while to warm up when we start to run. I believe it's the way our minds work, too: slow to get going. Such introverts take time getting along with people who they already know, if they meet after a long time.

However, for simplicity and consistency we will use the term introvert for someone who feel better when they aren't around people and who need to spend time with themselves to feel energized.

Even people who do understand introversion still imagine that introversion is really just about, you rather be on your own or with a close friend. Actually, there's so much more than that. I am an introvert; people think that I am shy, I always want to be alone, people think I am not fun to be with. They even feel that I don't like people; I don't like being with my friends, actually these all are some common myths. In reality, I like spending quality time with my friends, I prefer eating in company with people I am really close to else I will just eat by myself.

Many introverts find themselves really close to the nature, introverts like parking their car near trees, they like being in connection with the nature, it just sounds good to them. One of the possible reasons to this can be if they are in a social interaction and they come back to get their car in the parking lot the nature will help them to recharge the drained energy. If you are an introvert and you want to challenge yourself; try dining with people whom you don't know, because the whole idea of challenging yourself is to come out of the comfort zone and such a situation won't let you be comfortable for too long.

We, introverts are not superior or better than extroverts nor we are inferior it is just like choosing to a certain kind of food, like some people are vegetarians and vegans and some prefer being meat eaters. Also, I like to avoid debates with people, as I hate long
conversations. Ilet others say things that don't even make sense but I let them talk fearing that if I say something that will turn into a discussion, which I would avoid at any cost. Most of the time I know the answers to the questions asked in the classes or lectures but I won't answer because in order to answer I would have to speak up; and the conversation is something that I want to avoid. I would instead murmur the answer in my friend's ear and will repent when theteacher acknowledges my "friend's correct answer".

Another thing that excites me is to write exams and dairy to express a part of myself, text people instead of calling to communicate with friends on social media and emails instead of meeting them in person. Introvert or Extrovert, it is never 100%, people lean one way or the other.I am someone who usually doesn't like songs,I mean I don't like the words, I instead like music without the lyrics. I don't like anyone shouting in my head. The voice of a violin is far soothing to my ears than a human yelling in the air close to my ears. I am a little bit sensitive, however at times I like being sarcastic. At times, Ihave observed that I don't realize if someone is being rude or mean to me. It is only when someone asks me about the incident that why didn't I give them a befitting reply,it's only then when I realize I was being treated meanly. Talking about myself, I am a big ball of fun, I may be shy to strangers or the ones whom I am not very comfortable with, but in contrast, my closest friends believe that I am hilarious, I am funny and without me our group is lifeless.

In order to gel up with extroverts and grow
 professionally I had to do some tasks half-heartedly like learning small talks, looking at social side of things, I forced myself to talk to people. Similarly, other people do a lot of things to try being lesser of an introvert and more of an extrovert by watching other people, learning things from them like interacting skills and the way they glibly talk to strangers and do the kind of stuff which is really hard for introverts, copying other workers and seeing how they present their work to their bosses and superiors. People try to take tips and searching the web to improve their communication, presentation and people skills. What I learnt from being in corporate world is, how to say "no" and how to question what sounds illogical, saying "no" shows your

assertive side and asking for clarifications and logic shows your inquisitive side. There are a few more things that the introverts have to experience in their day to day life, like they feel nervous in unfamiliar places, with unfamiliar people, there are times when they talk to strangers and they feel as if they are eating grass. There are situations when we do not feel comfortable, like meeting people with different wavelength and vibes which prevent us from making a connection and continuing a conversation with them. Some people have altogether a different vibe which comes between to start a conversation. These energy level differences are other barriers that come across us. It doesn't matter how attractive you are, if you don't start the conversation I won't, it's not like I don't want to, but I just can't.

One thing we need not worry about is being an introvert It's not a disorder or a disease. I have seen people take

personality test - to see why they are the way they are - why are they doing what they like doing; why they like things, which they do and why they dislike things, which theydon't like. Some of the things that introverts like doing are not socializing, non-negotiable self-time, no interruptions when they are doing something. Alone time, is their recharging time; like lunch break, mornings when theydon't have to say a word and they can relish on their food, enjoy their thoughts and the food of course. We introverts try avoiding bigger events and try to reduce the intensity of the meetings, we say that we will grab coffee with them some other day instead of promising on spending the whole day with   them.
 The tricks that introverts use to be a little bit more comfortable at social gatherings are, dropping by earlier to get themselves acquainted with the place and the surroundings, shop online to avoid human interactions, buying grocery from a less

busy store where chances of meeting known people are lesser, taking different routes wherever they go occasionally so that they don't have to see the same people repetitively.

Chapter 2: Is Being An Introvert Wrong?

Going through the life of Mr. John, we learnt some things that will be relevant to this discussion, and we think sharing those lessons will be beneficial to you. This is because, sharing it will aid our discussion of this topic and as well enhance your reasoning of whether being an introvert is right or wrong. Are you ready for the journey? Great! Ready? Perhaps we should ask the following question to set our journey on motion.

WHO IS MR. JOHN?

No one knows him more than he knows himself, but few call him an introvert. Very few people who understand the pattern of life of an introvert know that Mr. John is a real introvert, a complete introvert. Other people only see him as a proud, selfish and an antisocial fellow. They see him as a fellow who does not like people. The reasons: Mr. John does not like being among people, he talks where there are not so many people and suddenly goes silent when people start to gather; and they think he does not make friends. But the facts are: Mr. John like people, he only feels more comfortable in living a private life, and he make friends, he just does not make too many friends. End of the journey! Now let's return home.

There is nothing wrong in being an introvert. Many people think it is wrong because they know very little about introverts. There are many myths about them. I believe you know myths are stories with no facts. For instance, in the above anecdote, two of the myths about Mr. John are: he does not like people and he is proud. Relying on those false assumptions, those people misunderstand being an introvert as being wrong. They see introversion as an attitude that is deliberate. There are so many people like those, so many people who know little about introverts. However, those are as wrong as their assumptions.

17

As it can also be seen in the anecdote, there are very few people who know whom Mr. John is. Those will certainly not spread those myths, for they know how introverts live. To them, being an introvert is not the same as being proud or nursing a hatred for people. It is a choice of life. Those will see introverts as special fellows with distinctive characters, and there is nothing wrong in being special, there is nothing wrong in being different from others. So, judging whether being an introvert is wrong or right depends on individuals and their masteries of them, as there is nothing wrong in living a quiet life. Should we say Mr. John is wrong or right living that way? No! He is not wrong. Everyone is privy to his or her own life.

However, there are some common mistakes that introverts make. Some are as follow.

COMMON MISTAKES EXHIBITED BY INTROVERTS

Appearing unfriendly: Introverts present themselves to others as fellows who do not care about them. Not all introverts are cold-hearted, but most of them show similar traits in the way they present themselves to others. As an introvert, you may be a warm-hearted fellow but no one will know that unless you show them. Introverts can do better by improving on the way they appear to people. Appear less unfriendly. That way, people will hold on little to some of the erroneous beliefs held against you.

Introverts hardly ask for help: Unless they are at edge of a cliff, introverts rarely seek people's help, and that sometimes may be dangerous. The reason why people see introversion as a bad thing is because they believe introverts live a risky life. Even at their own detriment, introverts are usually willful when it comes to solving their own problems. As an introvert, seeking people's help will not make you less a human, it will rather strengthen your relationship with them.

Introverts do not always stand for others: People call introverts selfish because they hardly stand in for others. Other introverted fellows rarely stand for themselves too, especially on the issues related to their rights. Introverts would rather sit and be cheated than standing. This mistake could be corrected too.

Introverts prefer people initiating a conversation with them: Introverts would not talk to you first. They will want you to approach them first, and such attitude is always being misinterpreted as pride. However, an introverted person could do more than that by chatting people up first.

Chapter 3: So Are You An Introvert Or An Extrovert? - How To Know For Sure

So many things have been said about what makes someone an introvert. The problem is, not everyone knows whether they are introverts or not. There are people who get so confused about who they are that they forget to really reflect on their lives—on what they want, what they hate, what applies to them and what makes them tick.

There are vast differences between introverts and extroverts. To help you understand these differences better and to help you know whether you are an introvert or not, take a look at the chart below.

Introverts	Extroverts
-Can develop relationships slowly -Comfortable	-Acts before thinking -Always happy to share their thoughts and ideas with others

on his own; craves solitude -Communicates better in writing or by means of gestures -Concentrates on things -Does not like too much attention -Doesn't like crowds too much -Focused on their "own world" -Is sometimes idealistic -Likes keeping their ideas to themselves -Likes routine	-Are enthusiastic and happy when there are a lot of people around -Becomes bored quickly -Comfortable working with groups -Finds it easy to talk to others -Has a wide circle of friends and enjoys a wide range of activities -Known as a people's person/is outgoing -Known as the "soul of the party" -Sometimes has hard time concentrating/thoughts aren't collected -They don't like repetitive tasks

-Likes to do things on his own (such as projects, eating alone, etc) -Likes to know only few people -Reserved and Reflective -Some control the amount of love they give -Thinks before acting	

If you can relate to more of the statements on the left side of the chart than those on the right side, you are most likely an introvert. There's nothing wrong with it—accept that you are one and you'll see that things will be lighter and easier for you.

Chapter 4: Definition Of An Introvert

You have heard the term introvert, and maybe you have suspected that you may be one. In this chapter we are going to dive into the self-preserved world of an introvert and find out exactly what it means to be one.

Even though many people think that defining a person as an introvert is a simple task, when they actually confront this type of person it can be unclear at times if he or she is in fact an introvert. They sometimes mistake an introverted person as being rude, impolite, and arrogant. The reality of it is that introverted people seem this way due to their innate personality traits and do not mean to behave in such manners. These people do not hold their heads high, and they do not automatically think you are an uninteresting person -- it is just who they are.

Here is how to tell if a person you may be interacting with is an introvert, or conversely, if you possess qualities of an introvert.

● They have fewer friends: An introverted person has fewer friends than most of other people. This is due to the fact that they do not need to surround themselves with many people and are perfectly content with being alone. They do enjoy company, but typically it is of smaller numbers of people who they know well. Relationships that are formed with introverts are typically deep and very meaningful. Although other members in their immediate circle of friends may also be introverts, extroverts may be included as well.

● They are cautious and look for purpose: This is another main characteristic of introverts. They need a reason in order to react when in a situation. When an introvert finds a reason, this person will think first about their response, and they

25

will then, and only then, react to the situation accordingly. They typically do not do anything to harsh or drastic – at least not right away.

• They may seem lonely, but they are not: Introverted people often times spend time alone and they will use their time very effectively. They will explore the depths of their own thoughts and seek the roots of their emotions. Many extroverts interpret this as an uncommon behavior and may think the introvert is just a lonely person; however, they are completely wrong. They love and cherish their introspective alone time.

• Introverts can make good leaders: Although introverts are not "people's people", they can prove to be good leaders; however, they must lead those who are self-starters. Despite the popular belief that an introvert cannot run things because they are too quiet, under the right conditions they can actually be the best to lead people. If the group were full of self-starters, the introvert would be able to pull the group's potential to the front and help them grow. It is only when the group actually needs loudness and a spark that is provided by an extrovert, that the introvert may face challenges in leadership.

• They are typically the last to raise their hand: An introvert in a group setting would probably be the very last to raise their hand to answer a question – that is if they'd raise their hand at all. Think back to your days in elementary school, how often did you raise your hand? Extroverts often times are ready and eager to raise their hand in order to stand out during social situations, but more than likely introverts are not comfortable being called upon.

• Introverts are more likely to wear headphones in public environments: Whether it is making their way through a crowd at a bus station or walking through a crowd on the street, introverts do not seek contact with other people. In past decades, if you didn't want to interact with others, you would have to keep your head down and look ahead, or hold an open book. Today, introverts have technology to help them avoid interacting with strangers.

• Introverts do not like to engage with those who are upset or angry: An introvert is more likely to avoid those who seem like they may be in a bad mood. Research conducted by the University College of London psychologist, Marta Ponari, and other collaborators, shows that those with high introversion failed to show the "gaze cuing effect". Typically, a person would see a face on a screen that is looking in a direction, and then the person would follow the gaze; being the cue. An introvert will not look if the person seems to be upset.

• An introvert normally receives more texts, calls, and emails than they make: Those that are highly introverted do not reach out voluntarily to others as frequently as others reach out to them. Most introverts will not make a call to pass time; this is voluntary socializing and they do not like to do this. In a similar way, they do not initiate emails; they typically only respond to those who have already emailed them. It is important to note, however, that introverts are more likely to choose to communicate via email or text message than in person or over the phone. It is quite likely that if you are an introvert, you will avoid jobs that would require you to reach out to others like telemarketing. If you were forced to invite people to a social event (if you even had one to begin with), you would more likely send your invite through the Internet or snail mail rather than call the person to invite them.

● Small talk to an introvert is not an option: Introverts will not strike up a conversation with people they know casually or not at all. It is almost impossible for an introvert to imagine him or herself as a person who will speak with a cashier about the storm outside, for example. If the introvert is stressed out or uncomfortable in any way, he or she normally does not tell or give a clue to this. The introvert may feel like it is not the business of those around him or her.

While being an introvert comes with its challenges, it definitely has its advantages as well. For example, an introvert is far less likely to make a mistake in a social situation, such as inadvertently insulting another person whose opinion is not agreeable. An introvert would enjoy reflecting on their thoughts, and thus would be far less likely to suffer from boredom without outside stimulation. The only risk that an introvert will face is that people who do not know them may think that you are aloof or that you think you are better than them. If you learn how to open up just a little bit with your opinions and thoughts, you will be able to thrive in both worlds. You can then stay true to your personality without appearing to be antisocial. This book aims to help you with that.

Chapter 5: Introverts Versus Extroverts

A crucial step in surviving as an introvert is to understand what introversion is about and to appreciate the assets and strengths you possess because you are an introvert. In order to manage, you must first understand. Therefore let's first look at some basics and the key differences between introverted people and extroverts. Introversion means preferring the inner world, thinking about ideas and wanting to understand, while extraversion means preferring the outer world, including people, things and a desire for action.

Introversion and extroversion made simple

Introversion and extroversion concern where we get our energy. This is important to grasp because it's the key to the differences in behavior between introverts and extroverts:

• Extroverts get their energy from interaction with people and things; the outer world, in other words. Extroverts are energized by interaction and tend to be much more animated and expressive than introverts. They enjoy being with people; many extroverts can talk with people all day long and still look forward to a group gathering in the evening.

• Introverts get their energy internally; much of their communication takes place on the inside, a private place not accessible by others. Thus, they are often less talkative, animated and expressive. Introverts lose energy from interaction. The very process of talking — or even listening — for an ex- tended period depletes an introvert's energy. As a result, introverts have a strong need for Cave

Time to recharge. The impact of this difference in where we get our energy is significant because it influences how we communicate, when we communicate, and what we communicate about.

• Extroverts typically think out loud. All that talking is actually the thought process in action. It's not surprising, therefore, that extroverts sometimes seem to change their minds in mid-sentence as they work through their ideas and draw conclusions.

• Introverts, by contrast, tend to process their thoughts internally before voic- ing them — if indeed they voice them at all. Introverts often prefer time to reflect before speaking. As a result, they may take longer to respond than extroverts, but may be more articulate when (if!) they do respond; after all, their utterances have been through several rehearsals already.

Behavioral patterns of Introverts

• Introverts seek depth over breadth. They like to dig deep—delving into issues and ideas before moving on to new ones. They are drawn to meaningful conversations—not superficial chit-chat—and know how to tune in and listen to others.

• They prefer writing to talking. On the job, they opt for e-mail over the telephone and stop by only when necessary. They are averse to excessive conversation and many gravitate toward social networking Web sites such as LinkedIn, Facebook, and Twitter.

• They are usually quiet, reserved, and low-key. They have no desire to be the center of attention, preferring instead to fly below the radar. Even in heated conversations or circumstances, they tend to stay calm—at least on the outside—and to speak softly and slowly.

• Introverts can experience "people exhaustion" that results in an assortment of ailments at work—headaches, backaches, stomachaches, etc.—yet feel fine off the job.

The important thing is that one personality type is not cooler than the other type – be it extrovert, introvert or any of their subtypes. You can find very successful and happy people on both sides. It doesn't matter if you're an introvert or an extrovert, the key is to understand yourself better and build your life on your strengths. Nevertheless, when being an introvert hinders you, you have to go out of your comfort zone and push yourself to become better.

The good news is that when you push yourself to overcome weaknesses of one type or the other at key moments in your life that need characteristics of the opposite side, you may slowly become the ambient type, possessing both introvert and extrovert personality traits; then you can experience the benefits of both types and make your experience and understanding of life much richer and deeper, probably also loving and getting along with more people. As an introvert, make sure that introspection and your inner world work to your own benefit. Use your introversion to build a superior life strategy based on a better understanding of how life works. As an introvert, you probably also have an incredible capacity to analyze, prioritize ideas and connect them to an environment, thinking through what it would take to realize them.

Chapter 6: What Is Introversion?

Before going into greater detail about how you can become a bit more extroverted, you must first learn more about your introversion. Some people mistakenly believe that introverted people are just overly shy; they think that they do not like to mingle with others because they are afraid that they would just embarrass themselves. This is not entirely true though.

Though it is true that most introverts are shy, that does not mean they cannot handle themselves in social gatherings, it's just that they rather dislike them. If you are not sure if you are just overly shy or if you are a true introvert, check yourself if you have the following traits:

- You can actually interact with other people, you have no problems whatsoever going to social gatherings, but the thing is, you would rather stay at home and read a book.

- You are actually a good listener, but a good conversationalist you are not.

- You let your writing do more of the talking for you.

- You do not really care for fame and fortune.

- You do not like conflicts with other people, so you try your best to be on their good side.

- You would rather be in the company of a few good friends rather than being in a huge party.

- You always feel tired and irritable after you force yourself into social activities.

- You always make excuses not to go out with your friends.

If you find that most, if not all of these characteristics actually describe you well then you are a true introvert.

What are the differences between shyness and introversion?

You may think that the qualities mentioned above are also the same that describe how being painfully shy is like, and technically, you are right. However, an introvert and a shy person do not always share these qualities.

Most, if not all shy people suffer from social anxiety. This means that being in the presence of a large group of people, or even just the thought of it, is enough to make them quake in their boots. Fearing social interaction is different from not having interest in it. There are actually a lot of introverts who are not shy, and an equally large number of introverts who are shy.

It's okay to be an introvert

Do not think that introversion is such a bad thing; there are actually quite a number of positive qualities that introverts have that extroverts do not. For instance, though it is true that introverts do not have a very large social circle the same as extroverts do, they do tend to value their friends and acquaintances much more; this means they like making friends for life. Introverts are actually great workers because they need very little stimulation to encourage them to work hard. They do not need to hear praises from others to make them feel more motivated to work (although they do appreciate it when their superiors give them praises), in fact, they would rather work alone (they are actually more productive that way).

Another good quality that introverts have is that they are more sensitive to the feelings of the people around them. They know when the person in front of them suddenly feels uncomfortable, so they know when they need to back off and give him or her some space. Being the good listeners that they are, introverts also value the opinion of others, making them good leaders and managers because they know how to utilise their groups' skills, talents, and knowledge.

Did you know that some of the greatest minds in history were introverts? Albert Einstein, the brilliant physicist that came up with the Theory of Relativity, would lock himself in his study and ponder about how the world works and how best he could explain what he figured out. J.K. Rowling, the author of the world-famous Harry Potter book series, actually wrote the books in a quiet little coffee shop in London where she would usually sit alone and look over her notes. Other great introverts include, George Orwell, Charles Darwin, and the great painter Vincent Van Gogh, so you are really in good company.

Can you really become an extrovert?

Unfortunately, you cannot do a complete 180 and change from an introvert to an extrovert. If you are an introvert, chances are you will remain the same until the end of your days. However, you can learn to be more sociable, and somehow give a bit of balance between your introversion and the tiny amount of extroversion you have. What you actually want to happen is that you want to overcome your shyness, you want to learn how you can communicate well with other people.

It is not that you want to become the centre of the party all of a sudden; you just want to learn how you can socialise with other people without always having a huge shroud of dread hovering over your head. You want to learn how you can speak up your mind and avoid becoming a doormat for other people. If you want all of these things for yourself then this book is perfect for you.

Although you cannot get rid of your introversion completely, there is a way for you to become more extroverted. You can get rid of that crippling fear that you always seem to get whenever you find yourself in the middle of a huge crowd, and you can set yourself free from the shackles of shyness that prevent you from becoming the best person that you can be. Now that you understand more about yourself and your introversion, the next step is to learn more about your polar opposites, the extroverts.

Chapter 7: How Are Relationships Developed When You're Introverted

First, stop calling yourself an introvert.

Personality assessments in psychological studies provide great references for us to discuss their semantics and be able to understand each other's unique traits. However, by associating yourself so easily with a label, that actually provides the risk of you subconsciously trying to model yourself after its associated traits, as opposed to acting from your own unique intentions and emotions.

Because of classic social conditioning, we may subconsciously act into the roles that have been laid out for us. For example, just think of the various gender roles, cultural stereotypes, professional roles, and certain caricatures that we use to simplify the impressions we have of the various people we meet.

If you have always identified with being introverted, and believe that it has something to do with the success of your relationships, then a few things should be re-evaluated.

There is more to you than that.

As human nature is adaptable, it means that personality can actually change over time. This is the same way that confidence, skill and knowledge can be improved over time. Why do people identify themselves as introverts anyway? Here are some insights.

We have varying degrees of emotional strength and threshold. For some, socializing with people feels toxic or exhausting.

Some people get anxious and turned off by the difficulty of developing relationships, or dealing with incompatible personalities.

Some have no patience for small talk, or feel no profound purpose in surface-level conversations.

Communicating in-person feels difficult, and sometimes being online or on the phone is an easier method to speak with others.

Sometimes, being a hermit or being attached to things such as computers, technology, and other hobbies are simply comfort or avoidant mechanisms.

Low self-esteem and confidence can affect emotional strength, capacity for empathy, relationship management skills and solid perception of social interactions.

Some have difficulty communicating because of communication style, pattern, language or perception. Certain ideas or feelings have varying degrees of value and profoundness to different people.

And lastly, some people have suffered physical or emotional trauma, which has affected the way they manage emotions and relationships.

You must be careful with the titles and labels that you choose to associate yourself or others with. Your character is what you create for yourself, rather than a pre-structured concept that just happens to be widely known.

By starting with this context, you can begin your approach to socializing better by having more accountability over your own actions, thoughts and perceptions. Personality Types are great references for discussion, but by no means should you use them as an excuse for your decisions, such as a reason to not act or change. They do not define who you actually are.

By acknowledging this personal accountability, you are forced to be more emotionally present in every unique situation and relationship. This will enable you to act through your own genuine intentions, feelings and motivations.

Chapter 8: Am I Introverted - Or Just Shy?

Do you screen your phone calls? Do you need lots of alone time to feel rested? Do you avoid awkward small talk? Would you rather be relaxing on the couch, rather than out networking at a large work event? Does the word "networking" make you cringe a little?

You just might be an introvert.

What It Means to Be an Introvert

There's a surprising amount of disagreement on what we mean when we talk about introversion. Let's start with a short list of what introversion is NOT:

- shyness
- social phobia
- passive aggression
- narcissism
- misanthropy
- agoraphobia
- avoidance disorder
- aloofness

- low self-esteem

Can you be an introvert who is a bit on the shy side? Sure. But you can also be an introvert who feels quite at ease in social situations. Can you be an introvert with a strong sense of self-confidence? Yes! On the opposite hand, you can also be an introvert who lacks confidence. Wherever you are in your life right now, just know that it's okay to lean toward the introvert side of the spectrum. Let's peel back the layers on what it means to be an introvert.

Over the years, I've read dozens of books, hundreds of articles and interviewed researchers in search of a perfect definition that encapsulates the experience of being an introvert. What I found is that there are dozens of definitions – and no "perfect" definition.

Carl Jung described an introvert as a person who tends to be more inward turning (toward inner thoughts, feelings and moods), while extroverts tend to be outward turning (toward social interactions).

The most commonly accepted definition — and the one I use in this book — is that an introvert is a person who gains energy from spending ample time alone, while an extrovert gains energy by interacting with others. Keep in mind that introversion exists on a spectrum, so while I might consider myself to be deeply introverted, you might only consider yourself to be mildly introverted.

In any case, if you're an introvert, chances are you:

- tend be attuned to your feelings and moods
- need ample time alone to recharge
- sometimes have trouble coming up with on-the-spot answers to questions (hence, my Skype interview stress)
- have a high degree of self-awareness
- are more reserved in large groups or unfamiliar settings
- enjoy learning through observation

- tend to be more outgoing among close acquaintances
- pick friends carefully
- prefer one-on-one connection to large groups
- need downtime to "recharge" after social events

Sound familiar? If you feel a glimmer of recognition when reading this short list, welcome to the tribe.

If you look closely at this list, you'll notice that these sub-traits are all (for the most part) pretty desirable. Who wouldn't want to be highly self-aware, observant, and feelings-attuned individual?

The trouble comes when the introvert meets the world — a world that often places high value on exuberance, speed and high visibility. No doubt about it, it's tough out there for an introvert. But I've been taking notes and developing practical, actionable steps that can help you thrive no matter where you find yourself. Let's get to work.

Chapter 9: Shyness Vs. Introversion

Understanding Introversion

Introversion is a natural characteristic. It defines who you are on the inside. It dictates how you find fulfillment in the world around you. And that fulfillment is not out there. It is inside. This is the reason introverts spend so much time alone.

This is not to say introverts hate being with others. We do like it. But we try to limit the amount of time spent in the company of friends or relatives. Otherwise, our energy reserves get drained.

Extroverts, on the contrary, find fulfillment in being with other people. Keep them alone for too long, and they will start complaining about it.

To an introvert, however, the same situation would be a blessing. It hands him the opportunity to sit in silence and enjoy the random thoughts of his mind. How is the world made? How do phones work?

For other introverts, listening to music, reading a book, watching a movie, or playing a game is all that's needed to bring fulfillment.

For this same reason, introverts are rarely bored. They can stay at home all day and they will still be happy. The things that turn them on are readily available and do not take much energy.

Extroverts, on the other hand, need more stimulation. While they may enjoy watching a movie, it is better to watch it in a room full of people.

Another thing that differentiates introverts are the topics they like to talk about. Usually, it's things they are passionate about. While they may discuss anything with anyone, topics considered uninteresting are unrewarding and tax the system.

But our society is bent. We see introversion as a problem. No wonder research has found that we rank fast and frequent talkers as more competitive, likable, and smarter. This is madness. Would you say having a large head means you are smarter? Or that having a loud voice means you are a great singer?

Some of the world's most influential people are introverts. You can think of Bill Gates, Albert Einstein, and J.K Rowling as examples. Actually, research shows that close to half of people in the world are introverts.

But this has not stopped others from pressuring introverts to become extroverts. You probably are aware of phrases like:

You should go out more

You should come out of your shell

You should try to have more friends

You should try to have some fun

But trying to change yourself from an introvert into an extrovert is like denying your true identity. If you are short, then you are short. If you are green, then you are green. If you are an introvert, you are an introvert. Instead of fighting what you are, learn how you can use it to your advantage. You can achieve a lot by focusing on your strengths rather than fixing your weaknesses. And by the way, being an introvert is no weakness.

The level of introversion varies. No one is 100% introverted and no one is 100% extroverted. We all have characteristics of both personalities. However, these characteristics differ in intensity. I may be more introverted than you are. But we are still both introverts.

A better way to understand this is to imagine there is a spectrum. On one end is introversion and on the other is extroversion. Those close to the middle are called ambiverts (people who show equal characteristics of introversion and extroversion). And most people lie in this region.

While you would believe that those at the far ends of this spectrum would be pure introverts or extroverts, such individuals do not exist. Carl Jung famously said that such men would be lunatic asylums. And it's easy to understand why he would make such a statement. Your life is multi-dimensional. And to live it to the fullest, you need to take care of all things that matter. You cannot stay locked up in your room without any sort of human interaction. You will go insane in the end. You need to see other people. You need to talk to them and have fun with them.

Likewise, you cannot keep on looking on other people for fulfillment all the time. There will come a time when you will need to focus on yourself. You need to get in touch with your feelings and your thoughts. No one will do this job for you. This helps you understand yourself, from the things you love to your purpose in life. Equipped with this understanding, you can better decide how to interact with other people.

Understanding Shyness

Shyness and introversion are usually confused as being one and the same. But it is a mistake to think extroversion means you are not shy. I have seen a lot of shy extroverts. And I know a lot of introverts who are not shy. Again, Bill Gates is an example.

Research shows that shyness and introversion share the same symptoms. And probably, this may be the origin of the confusion.

When we talk of shyness, we refer to a fear that you have towards people. You have a mindset that whoever you meet is judging you. You feel that there is something inadequate about you. And you avoid people so they don't see your flaws. You are convinced that if they do, they will banish you from their circles. And you will be left alone in this world.

This is an instinctive characteristic that has lived with humans for very long. You must remember that before we had cities, we lived in jungles. Danger was at every turn. With inadequate tools to use in defending ourselves, sticking with others was the best way to survive. (Thankfully, others discovering your flaws in this age no longer equates to death.)

Shyness is a big problem. You want to connect with others but because of your fear, you do not. So you keep on living a solitary life, while a part of you longs for the outside world.

This is unhealthy. You will find your life unfulfilling. And it may drive you into doing unwanted behaviors. For example, most people who find themselves in such situations indulge in extreme shopping. They believe looking wealthy will win them the love of people.

Not only is shyness a problem to you, but it also affects how others see you. For example, a study found that women find shy men unattractive.

On a similar track, another study by the University of Wisconsin at Madison discovered that shy men have low chances of winning a job, getting married, or having kids.

And this is easy to understand why. If you act nervously at a job interview, the employer will obviously consider you a bad fit. If you are afraid to meet potential lovers, chances of getting married or having kids diminish.

Myths about Introverts

As it turns out, most things we believe about introverts are not real. People look at the characteristics of introversion and make conclusions. Here are some of the most common myths.

Introverts do not like people – introverts do like people. Just that when they are in social situations, they like to stick with those they know. Or they may chat with just a few strangers. Large groups of people are overwhelming to an introvert. They sap his energy, living him lifeless. This is why you may hear others saying introverts do not like going out.

Another reason introverts tend to stick to people they know is to avoid small talk. While most people hate it, the animosity runs deeper for introverts. They like to discuss topics they think matter.

Introverts do not like talking – another common misbelief because introverts do love talking. It is just that before they open their mouths, they like to think about the words they are about to say. So most times, they do not talk a lot for the sake of filling silence gaps.

In addition to this, introverts are great listeners. They value what others have to say. And they are deeply interested in learning. This helps them mold their responses so they are in line with what others are saying.

Introverts don't like fun – nothing could be more wrong than this. And this shows how twisted we have become in society. Usually, the definition of having fun these days is going to parties, being talkative, and meeting new people. While introverts are capable of doing all these things, they cannot do them for too long.

An introvert's ideal way of having fun is to spend time in solitude doing something he values. And meeting new people or going to parties is usually bottom on the list. Like I already said, reading books, watching movies, listening to music, or even cooking may be all that's needed to have fun.

Introverts do not make great leaders — being a great leader does not mean you should be loud, or talk too much, or have an outgoing personality. While these characteristics are important, they are not the only things that define a great leader. As for networking, which is important for any leader, introverts can act more extroverted when the situation calls it.

And the good listening skills of introverts mean they take the input of others seriously.

So introverts do make great leaders. Take Mahatma Gandhi as an example. In fact, a poll by US Today found that as much as 40% of leaders are introverts.

Introverts are smarter than extroverts – just because introverts are capable of coming up with great ideas does not make them better than extroverts. We have extroverts to thank for some of the greatest ideas and discoveries of the world. Research, however, suggests that most of these extroverts are creative when they tune into their more "reflective and introverted roles." In addition, remember that there is some introversion in every extrovert.

You can easily know an introvert – because most introverts are pressurized to act more extroverted, it is not easy to point an introvert with just a few interactions. If there is need for it, an introvert can be as loud and as talkative as an extrovert. However, when everything is done, he will still turn his focus on the inside.

Introverts are not good at public speaking – there is very little correlation between being an introvert and giving a great public speech. The things that induce the fear of public speaking are very different from the things that make one an introvert.

For example, when about to give a speech, you will worry about whether the audience will like you. You may fear that you will forget the words to say when on stage. You may even think of what may happen if you puke. Extroverts have the same fears. Watch a couple of TED Talks and you will learn that some of the greatest talks are by introverts.

Chapter 10: Learn To Accept Yourself

One of the most difficult things for many people is to accept that they are introverts, even if they know they are. After all, as we have pointed out, being an introvert is not popular. Many people try to justify their introverted behavior by saying: "So what if I don't like socializing? Doesn't mean I'm an introvert".

Most of us are not pure introverts or pure extroverts since we may have traits from both extremes. But generally, we fall towards one side or the other of the extrovert-introvert scale. How can you tell where you land? Here are some of the more common traits of an introvert:

-Although you consider yourself sociable, in social situations or gatherings, you often find yourself wishing you were at home or by yourself doing a solitary activity such as watching TV or reading.

-You find that you can express yourself better by writing letters rather than through verbal communication.

- You actively avoid conflict or confrontation with other people.

-You are not interested in external validators such as fame and wealth that other people actively pursue.

-Social interaction can leave you feeling tired and drained, and badly in need of recharging.

-Instead of going to a party or other social gathering, yowould rather pursue solitary activities such as going to the gym or staying home.

-You prefer to listen more and talk less.

-You would rather surround yourself with a small group of close friends and family instead of having a large social circle of acquaintances.

If you find that you have several or even all of these traits, then you are an introvert or at least lean more towards introversion than extroversion. But as we said, being an introvert is not a bad thing. In fact, there are many positive traits that introverts have, so you should learn to embrace it.

Although having extroverts for friends can be fun, it is also often exhausting. Extroverts always have to be the center of attention and have to be surrounded by people all the time. In fact, one of the worst things for them is to be alone since they usually dislike being in their own company.

Thus, you should learn to embrace being an introvert. You should not feel bad about it and you should not let others make you feel bad about it as well. But the peer pressure to conform to what extroverts want is very strong. After all, who would want to say no when they are confronted with the question: "Don't you want to have fun?" Communicating your desires to others can be an act of courage, but when you finally learn how to do it through continuous practice, you'll find yourself happier, healthier, and feeling less resentful of others who you perceive force you to do things you don't want to do.

Chapter 11: Are You An Introvert?

Over the years, introverts have been tagged loners, reclusive, shy and deemed unsuitable for leadership positions because of their perceived lack of charisma. But adult introverts are not the only ones who suffer from negative perception. Even today, introversion is being discouraged in children. A prime example of this is a scenario that many parents of introverts face regularly – their child's teacher has expressed concern because the child in question is not as outgoing as others or keeps to themselves. These complaints by well-meaning people in the child's life further drive home the message that there is something wrong, and unnatural about being an introvert.

Being perceived as quiet, delicate and odd shouldn't define introverts as weak, boring and extremely fragile people. There are a great many stellar qualities lurking deep within that calm exterior. There is a fun side to being an introvert too! Dig through the pages of this book and you'll discover this fun side, unlearning some traditional ideas about introverts along the way. If you're introverted, you're sure to uncover and enjoy incredible truths about your personality.

Are you an introvert?

To be candid, very few introverts have ever been asked that question. Instead, they are asked questions like:

'Why are you so quiet?'

'Don't you get bored and lonely?'

'Are you angry?'

'Do you ever have fun?'

'Do you have any friends?'

While these questions are tiring for introverts, it often comes out of a poor understanding of introversion. Therefore, the next section of this workbook is important. It will address what introversion is not.

What Introversion Is Not

Introversion is not depression

Unfortunately, introversion is often wrongly associated with depression. Because many introverts tend to keep to themselves and are energized by spending time alone, they are often labelled as depressed. When family members or friends tag introverts as depressed, this can be further isolating for introverts who generally already feel isolated. Yes, introverts can feel isolated, and this often stems from not being understood by the people who matter the most to them. While introverts can also suffer from depression, introversion and depression are entirely different.

Introversion is not being antisocial or asocial

Another common misconception when it comes to introversion is equating it with being antisocial. While it is possible for an introvert to be antisocial, the two states of mind are quite different. A major difference between an introvert and an antisocial individual is that an antisocial person behaves in a manner that is against social norms and which is also often harmful to those around them. In contrast, introverts are people who simply love their own company and get energized by spending time alone. Asocial individuals, on the other hand, dislike socializing and try to avoid it. Honestly, sometimes the lines between all these personalities blur so how do you know if you're an introvert?

Let's use a simple analogy to help you know for sure.

There are lots of things you can do with your phone. You can play games, chat with your friends, video call your grandparents, read an article, and work on the go. But first, you have to charge it fully, right?

For introverts, that charging happens when they're alone. They recharge their life batteries by spending time on their own. When their 'batteries' are full, they can engage in quite a number of activities. Even some activities which seem extroverted in nature. The difference, however, is that while an extrovert would be energized by spending time in highly stimulating environments like a large party, the introvert's 'battery' would be running down during that same party, and sooner rather than later. If you are always excited to go to events and then get tired before they're even halfway through, you just might be an introvert.

Introversion is not synonymous with being rude

While every introvert has a unique personality, one behavioural trait common in this group is their inability to tolerate small talk. They are not deliberately being rude but tend not to have the ability to sustain conversation that doesn't seem important. This and other factors may be construed as rudeness. It does not mean that an introvert cannot be rude, but rudeness shouldn't be considered synonymous with being an introvert.

What is an introvert?

Now that we know what introversion is not, let us briefly look at what introversion is.

Introversion is the compelling need to enjoy one's own company and solitude. Introverts are more likely to engage themselves in activities that encourage introspection.

Introverts enjoy activities like writing, reading, pet sitting, painting, watching videos online for hours, visiting libraries, museums or art theatres and meditating. These activities require minimum stimulation and interaction with other people.

Introverts are often thoughtful people. They are much likely to thoroughly think things through before speaking.

When it comes to friends, introverts prefer quality over quantity. They prefer small groups of friends to large groups.

Being around lots of people drains the energy of introverts.

Introverts are usually quiet. This is often related to the 'energy' issue. When introverts deem a conversation as not deep or meaningful, they tend to remain quiet and avoid it.

Introverts learn by observation. Unlike extroverts who are more likely to learn by trial and error, introverts learn best by watching.

Introverts prefer jobs that allow for independence. Jobs that require lots of social interaction and team effort are usually not of interest to introverts as they prefer working alone.

Chapter 12: Introversion And Extroversion

Have you ever gone to a seminar or a talk where the speaker or the host tries to engage the crowd in a motivational activity? Did you feel excited and energized, or did you try to think of a way to get out of such a tedious and needless activity?

If you belong to the latter group, then there just might be a good chance that your personality leans toward introversion. You need to remember to never let yourself be isolated or feel like an outcast in such activities that require a certain amount of cooperation and interaction. You don't get particularly thrilled by things like this; you simply get yourself energized or happy doing other things.

What does being an introvert mean?

Carl Jung, who was a Swiss psychiatrist and psychotherapist, and also the founder of the school of analytical psychology, popularized the term. Derived from the psychological aspects of personality (physical, mental, emotional, moral, social and spiritual), he stated that there are two different attitudes toward life.

According to Jung, a person who has an introverted attitude prefers to write, read and think freely. Although they enjoy and engage in socializing, introverted people prefer to do it in smaller groups or with close friends. In addition, introverts have an innate flow of personal energy or "vibe" around them—a perk focusing on subjective thoughts.

There are advantages and disadvantages to being an introvert. Some common disadvantages of introverted people include: A tendency to appear unfriendly, timid and uncertain. Some confidence issues when it comes to relating to people - especially relating closely. The advantages or the strengths of introverted people are also worth mentioning. Introverts are commonly known as great thinkers. And when it comes to thinking, Jung proposes that they see things in deeper meaning and understanding compared to extroverted people.

The reasons are:

- Introverted people think less of how the world sees them, but instead focus on how they can look at the world differently. It means that they are more concerned with the bigger picture and do not have the time to involve themselves in petty misconceptions and shallow points of view.

- Introverts are not solely focused on facts. They are more open-minded than others and have a great sense of forward thinking.

These innate traits among introverts have paved the way for outstanding free thinkers and probably the most brilliant minds across history. There are a lot of known introverts who turned out to be the most influential mathematicians or renowned philosophers of their time.

Even when it comes to "feelings," introverts have a rational way to weigh most things and see everything properly, almost as if they possess a genuine wisdom and a practical way of dealing with socializing. Although it may seem impractical to extroverts, introverted people have a well-developed thinking pattern that influences even their deepest emotions.

Jung enumerated the following about introverts and how they value their feelings and of those of other people:

- Some introverts become musically gifted, genuinely creative and in touch with their spiritual sides.

- Introverts may seem a bit distant, but in reality, they are filled with so much compassion and empathy toward their closest friends.

- Introverted people tend to be extremely reliable.

It is no surprise that introversion has produced the most prolific writers, talented dramatists, compassionate nurses, and outstanding psychologists known to man. This is because they are well in touch with the way they feel and have incorporated it into their goals and passions in life.

In comparison, what is an extrovert?

If introverts have an innate inward flow of personal energy, extroverts have an outward flow of personal energy. Since extroversion and introversion have a somewhat yin and yang relationship, the two are bound to be exact opposites. But at the same time, they are also naturally interwoven with each other.

People who are extroverts get themselves pumped up or energized by engaging in socially lively encounters. Extroverts prefer being in groups, parties, and other large social events. Being alone, or having a sense of solitude, is not preferred. Some researchers state that an inability to embrace the comfort of solitude might hinder their productivity and ultimately affect the creative process.

Just like how introverts possess different advantages and strengths, it is also the same with extroverts. The most commonly known trait of an extrovert is exceptional social skills. Extroverts approach any social event with striking confidence. Meeting new people is never a tedious task, but rather an opportunity to widen the social network and give a good impression toward a new acquaintance or a future confidante.

If you find yourself lost after reading the above descriptions because you don't fit either classification perfectly, that's okay. There are also some people who identify as ambiverts.

Simply put, ambiversion deals with people having almost equal amounts of introversion and extroversion in their personality, without either one being clearly dominant. These people are said to have the best of both worlds, because they can control their extroversion or introversion at will and adapt accordingly to the situation at hand.

Carl Jung once said that there is no such thing as a pure introvert or a pure extrovert. He even added that if a person like that existed, it would be something of pure insanity.

Chapter 13: Set Your Personal Goals

Introversion is not a weakness; it simply means that you are more comfortable being alone than in a group. You do not feel sad, lonely, or insecure when you're by yourself. In fact, many introverts say that they are at their happiest when they're alone. It does not mean that you do not have the necessary social skills to become successful.

Merely thinking about improving their social skills is usually enough to overwhelm most introverts. Introverts usually think that they need to become the life of the party, be the most popular person in the group or talk a lot of people to become successful, and this is just not the case.

You can have great communication skills just by being your normal self. Extroverts have the urge to keep the conversation going. They are not shy when it comes to initiating interactions. From the introvert's point of view, most of these interactions are pointless. This is the reason why they do not actively seek them out.

If you want to develop your communication skills and widen your professional network, you need to see the value of these seemingly unimportant interactions. To do this, you need to set your personal goals:

Your Goals

If you are a goal-driven person, you may already have your own short-term and long-term goals. If you do not have goals yet, you should take the time right now to develop them. You should create the following.

1.Decide what you want to accomplish with your life. You should list at least three things. These three things will become your lifetime goals.

2. Set three goals for the year that will help you reach your lifetime goals. These will become your annual goals.

By setting your goals, you be better able to identify the 'non-introvert' skills that you need to work on. This way, you will begin to value of networking and engaging more as these networking skills will help move you in the direction of your personal goals.

Focusing on your goals

After developing your personal goals, you should develop a system for reminding yourself of your goals.

1. Write your goals in your planner or your journal

If you use a planner, you may write your personal goals in it. You should dedicate one whole page for this activity. You should then look at your goal statements every morning before you start your day. Doing so will remind you of the things that you want to accomplish. This will lead you to decide to do actions that will help you reach your goals. If you do these actions consistently, you will be closer to your goals every day.

2.Use a vision board

A vision board is the visual representation of your goals. You would collect pictures or motivation quotes to be assembled on your vision board. You can then use a simple cork board and pin images these images that remind you of your goals on it. Hang this board somewhere in your room or office where you can always see it.

Remember to change the images in your vision board every three months at the very least. If you do not change them, your eyes will become accustomed to the images in your room or your office, and by then they will no longer inspire you to pursue your goals. People end up forgetting about their vision boards after a few months. By updating your images occasionally, you keep the contents of the vision board fresh.

Set the actions that you need to take to reach your goals

Now that you have a method that will constantly remind you of your goals, the next thing you need to do is decide on the specific actions required to reach your goals. If you want to start a business, you need to identify the requirements for starting it and the steps that you need to take to meet these requirements.

For your long-term goals, you may find that you might not even know what steps you need to get started, and this is normal. Just set these tasks aside for now until you gain the knowledge you need. You may create vague action plans for long-term goals if there are still some details lacking. You should fill the plan with more specific steps when you gain the information that you need.

For your short-term goals however, you should already have all the necessary steps to accomplish it. The more detailed your action plan is, the better your chances of success will be.

Identify your weaknesses

After developing your action plan, you should identify your personal constraints for reaching the goals. More specifically, you need to identify your weaknesses related to introversion. Here are some of them:

1. Shyness

Because introverts prefer being alone and only keep a small circle of friends, they may not have enough confidence to start everyday conversations. If you need to interact with people regularly to reach your goals, you need to work on overcoming your shyness.

2.Underdeveloped social skill

Lack of practice in talking to people may lead to underdeveloped social skills, which includes those that you need to interact with others. Social skills also include a fully developed emotional stability that will allow you to deal with people with different personalities. These skills will come in handy for when you need to talk to your boss or if you need to manage your subordinates.

3.Lack of social connections to reach your goals

Most worthwhile goals require collaboration with other professionals. You are lucky if you already have all the social connections that you need to reach your goals. For most people however, there is a need to widen their social circles. We will discuss how you can do this in later chapters.

4.Performance anxiety that affects your professional life

Because most introverts avoid performing in front of groups of people, they dont developed skills on how to adequately cope with anxiety leading up to a performance. In extreme cases, some introverts freeze-up in front of a crowd. Others may even feel physiological effects, like stomach aches and migraines as their performance gets closer.

By identifying the key weaknesses that are preventing you from reaching your goals, you can know which skills you need to work on. We will discuss how you can eliminate these weaknesses and become a successful introvert.

Chapter 14: Probable Reasons Behind Introversion

Our body's physiology is said to play a role in the way we react to our environments and our degree of introversion or extroversion. Anatomically, the arrangement of neurons present in the brain region called the RAS (Reticular Activating System) is the determinant factor of the level of arousal in an individual. The RSA also determines the level of transitions between sleepiness and wakefulness. It is also responsible for controlling the amount of information one can absorb while awake. The RSA tackles environmental threats by increasing the level of an individual's arousal, making such an individual alerted and prepared to counter the threats. Every individual has a limit in terms of the degree of arousal. Naturally, some are more aroused than others. A psychologist (Hans Eysenck) assumed that about 15 out of hundred people are slightly aroused; they have low level of arousal naturally. The other 15 percent are said to be highly aroused while the remaining 70% fall in between the line. They are neither low nor high in their level of arousal.

According to Hans' theory, those that are naturally highly aroused are introverts. This is because chronically introverts are highly excited and tend to always seek for ways to excuse themselves from things happening around them. Due to their high level of arousal, they are mostly very sensitive and alert, thereby getting more information from the environment than an extrovert would get. Getting a lonely and quiet place to stay allows them to resonate with what they have been taught or learnt.

Aside from this arousal theory of extroversion by (Hans Eysenck), other factors that could be responsible for introversion include;

1. The nature of the environment one is raised

A child who was raised in a quiet and secluded area is most likely to become an introvert. Due to the calm nature of his surroundings, he might be more interested in studying his environment and reflecting on it rather than going out with friends for social activities.

2. Method of upbringing

Children that are always on their own either because of their parents' tight schedule or guardian's strictness have a high tendency of becoming introverts.

3. Past experiences

We all have had a share of embarrassing moments. Some get over it and move on with life, while others see it as an excuse to keep to themselves, especially when this embarrassment has to do with associating with others.

4. Hereditary and many more

A lot of introverted people got the trait from their parents. Not as if they like being on their own, they just can't help it and are always looking for reasons to stay away from people. When invited for a date or party, they will never forget the clothes that need to be laundered. Their private moments they can't trade for anything.

Distinct signs to identify if you or someone is an introvert

Some often assume they can easily identify an introvert when they come across them, but here is a fact; they might be wrong. If care is not taken, you might take an extrovert that is very reserved as an introvert. Likewise, staying indoor might necessarily not be a routine engaged in by introverts alone but also extroverts that desired to have a secluded time for specific reasons. However, to be sure that someone is an introvert, there are specific signs that one must look out for. And for those wondering if they fall on the introvert or the extrovert side, these signs or features can help in seeing a clear picture.

However, since an introvert is primarily someone who 'lives' more inwardly than outwardly, there are certain physical signs that are attributed to introverts that distinguish them from their extrovert counterparts who are usually bubbling when around people whether known or unknown.

Listed below are some personality traits of introverts.

• You tend to avoid typical conversations

Can you take a moment to flashback on your interaction with people around you? Are you the type that naturally feels that a minute of discussion with a friend, neighbor, college, or even family members are too much? Or you intentionally avoid specific places or individuals just because you don't want to talk or share your thought with them? If you fall into these categories, among others, you MIGHT be an introvert. However, it possible that you may have compelling reasons for not wanting to engage in conversation with others; that is required at times, even by extroverts. But sincerely and objectively probe your mind, if the reason you are keeping back from talking to people is that important or not. And if it's not, then you are undoubtedly an introvert.

• You only prefer to listen and not verbally engaging in conversation

Listening attentively is, no doubt, one of the unique qualities of a potential achiever and leader. This is evident, as we tend to see depicted in several motivational books. However, some people do listen to conversations but would prefer to say little in return. Some might even have viable and constructive ideas or responses to contribute to specific talk or discussions, but somehow, based on their nature or personalities, they still chose to keep quiet. This, means you are an introvert.

• Find it hard to associate with others

Have you ever heard someone said, "We don't like staying much around 'Z', he/she makes us feel we are not welcome around him/her." The above scenario might be because the person in question may not associate with relevant group or individual with the same enthusiasm made available to him/her. This might also be an indication that one may be an introvert. However, the continuous occurrence of such experience might end up keep existing and potential friends away from you.

• Always prefer to stay indoor

Are you the type that your friends frequently tell, 'You only come out of your house once in during a blue moon'? Such a question is not asked because they are trying to start a conversation with you; it is because they have realized that your act of secluding yourself in-house is more of nature than having some important to do indoor. Likewise, because of the availability of internet and technology in recent time, some might want to use this as a cover-up; saying they don't have to physically associate with other when a practical and probably faster way is available. Yes, they are right! But in situations where communicating with relevant individuals through online chatting or sticking with your TV is far more comfortable than physical engagement with others, the person in question may be an introvert.

• You keep your distance when out with friends

Despite having a day out with friends, some individuals still prefer to keep some distance between themselves and the main crew. Though this is often done stylishly to reduce the probability of others noticing. What do you call that? Are you the type that visits the cinema with friends and your choice of sitting position is some sit away from those you went there together? Then your probably exhibiting signs of an extrovert.

• If you associate with extrovert alone

Do you know an introvert with extroverts friends might be easily identified as an introvert? This is because the extrovert friends will mostly be the ones doing the talking most of the time, hence, filling the gap for their introvert counterparts. However, findings have shown that introverts rarely like having introvert friends like themselves. Though this may not be done unconsciously, it is believed that introverts that make friends with themselves have the tendency to experience boring friendship relationships compared to having extroverts as friends.

• You are often personified as a quiet individual

Though quite a handful of extroverts do have their quiet time, they sometimes prefer to stay low and reserved for some reason. But this is not the same for an introvert. An introvert doesn't just decide to stay quiet once in a while; it is mainly a normal and daily routine for them. Staying quiet comes with ease for them. And when they choose to talk with or to anybody, it's always straight to the point.

No, they don't meddle in time-wasting discussion; this is not because they hate someone, but they are naturally eager to get back to their private place physically or mentally. So, for someone that is constantly being told "you are too quiet, gentle and reserved" among others. You are probably an introvert.

• When you don't feel motivated and relaxed around people

Are you the type that feels drained or drained after spending just a while with people? Do you always tell yourself it's time to detach yourself from a gathering of people when you know you have not even spent up to the request time with them? When you answer this question objectively and with sincerity, you will have an accurate answer to whether you are an introvert or not. This is another question for you: when your friends come with huge enthusiasm, inviting you to go to the football field or the cinema with them, are you always eager to follow them? And probably you give reasons for not going, are the reasons always that cogent for you to stay away from fun? Nonetheless, this basis alone can't be used in judging whether one is an introvert or not; however, when these acts are becoming too consistent, it merely portrays you as an introvert.

• Independent execution of task gives you delight

How do you feel when you are given a task that is to be done with other individuals as a team? Do you prefer executing the job alone, even when you know getting the task done as an individual would be more stressful for you? This simply, is a typical trait of an introvert. It's always about limiting their interaction with others.

Likewise, other traits of introverts include an unmatched desire to learn things by watching, feeling distracted and unfocused around people, having few friends, and extremely being self-aware, among others. Though at this point, it is vital to note that introversion is definitely not a human defect nor a stigma. However, when it is managed well and appropriating, you can become someone to be sorted after; this is evident with the handful of introverts doing great exploit globally.

Chapter 15: Unleashing Your Strengths

If you choose to make your life a lot easier as an introvert, you may as well practice and apply a few things. Meditation does not always cut it, and sometimes you may want extra help with everyday challenges.

Listen closely to what others say

Introverts are usually branded as absent-minded daydreamers that do not know what is going on around them. This is because they feed on acquired information the way a wine connoisseur samples a Merlot. Truth be told, introverts are often the poorest listeners. In that case, it is essential for an introvert to exercise better listening. Take time to listen to the radio (since radio broadcasts are uninterrupted by "Wait, I didn't catch that) and try to analyze the words you picked up.

Get a little confidence boost

Apparently, introverts are not the best communicators. As much as we want them to admit it, introverts seem to have a dearth in forging interpersonal relationships solely because they lack a socializing function in them. Because of this lack, they seem to communicate less confidently than others. One way to solve this is by TALKING WITH PEOPLE. There's nothing much to it other than to engage in real-world conversations with other people. Does it sound difficult? Well, it does at first, but it gets easier every day. Practicing conversations on topics as simple as the weather can stimulate your socialization skills and allow you to become better at conversing with other people. If at first you are reluctant, you can always have someone right beside you to act as your talking buddy. Start with simple topics and work your way up to bigger and more complex issues. You would be surprised how much of an interesting person you would be to yourself and each another.

Go on solitary walks

Great minds work well when left alone. But when walking, they develop a lot of beautiful ideas. There is a sort of therapeutic characteristic of taking walks in the park or around the house. Not only is it great exercise, but some introverts find something meaningful out of taking casual, solitary walks. It's slower and you enjoy the hustle and bustle of nature with every step. You are taking all of it in, giving yourself a good view at how life should be enjoyed: slow and steady.

During your days off, might I suggest turning off the PC, going outside and setting your mobile phone to instrumental jazz music. You would feel more calm and relaxed and happier seeing that the mood keeps you afloat from all the stress.

Plan your day ahead

Introverts are normally guilty of being unorganized and it is because of this that they tend to miss important deadlines and lose sight of small but important objects (think about the keys you left on the pantry, you absent-minded fool!). Apparently, this is one weakness that puts introverts at a great disadvantage, but this is one simple issue that can always be resolved by having a planner. Now, we are not ostracizing you for your inability to perceive time as it ticks by, but at least a planner allows you to be more in tune with important dates for turning in output. In some way, planners help you to stick to a schedule, another activity most introverts are not good at. It's a matter of discipline really, and it is also about keeping your main priorities intact. Introverts are known for their indifference towards these conventions, but there are still those who are able to deliver in time and who still know where they put their keys.

The fact of the matter is that introverts have a bad sense of keeping a schedule, but it is something that is actually practiced every day – just like talking to random strangers for instance.

Take responsibility

Let's go back to one weakness an introvert is notoriously known for. Being unorganized creatures, people who are looking within, are unaware of every result that was sourced from their actions. In some way, introverts have a lack of regard for taking responsibility, and it comes with the fact that they would rather blame other people for their mistakes. We are not talking generally here, but there are cases when one doesn't feel like taking the brunt of a problem and asking others to be sacrificial lambs, and this is one quality that alienates introverts in the first place.

Egos can take the place of reason, and that is where the fatal flaw of being a lone wolf lies. As a result, people are turned off by your actions and dismiss you as another know-it-all trying to prove himself. This affects professional relationships as much as it obstructs you from functioning in pursuit of personal and organizational goals. At any rate, you may want to take the safe route by taking responsibility for whatever issue arises, as long as it relates to the nature of your work. I know it is hard to accept responsibility, but being people whose minds are more fixated towards reason, the best things you can do is to set your ego aside and take responsibility. Admit your mistakes and silently work your way towards redeeming yourself. Not many people can do it, so to see an introvert actually having the guts to admit a mistake, is something you won't see every day.

Take control of your mind

Now we come to the most important part of being an introvert: Having to manage that engine of a brain!

This is not to say that introverts are robots in their own peculiar way, but it says a lot about how much dilemma they encounter on a daily basis, starting with how to effectively control their heads.

Imaginative and innovative. These are two words that best describe an introvert. Yet these only serve to cover up a deeper struggle. Introverts have to battle themselves in order to open up to other people. They have within them a sort of goblin of sorts that does not allow free rein of one's thoughts.

Luckily, once an introvert takes control of this goblin, he is able to take control of how he deals with the outside world. For a start, that goblin is the reason why you are always reluctant to go out of the house and mingle with other people and it is also the reason why you put off any work. It suppresses your industrious side in favor of your lazier side.

So what should you do about it? Well, just ignore it. It doesn't do much good to keep it inside and it doesn't help to give it control over your life decisions either. Always remember that your life is what you make of it. You always have the choice of letting the goblin run your life, or free yourself from its control and take the high road towards success.

As reasonable as you are, you would probably pick the option that would give your life a whole lot of meaning.

Keep a journal

Living as an introvert can be difficult. You might have realized this earlier in this book, but it is true that introverts have it more difficult than most people. What with the loneliness and the constant struggle to socialize (even if you lack an understanding thereof), there is really much work before introverts can truly unleash the full capacity of their powers.

The road towards success for an introvert is one that takes several steps. It is also a journey filled with drama. So, we can say a lot about the maelstrom of emotions prevailing in an introvert's quest for self-realization. Come to think of it, it makes for a great deal of interesting content.

Keeping journals and recording your life's progress has some sort of therapeutic effect all on its own. For one, it's a great way for silent, inexpressive people to vent out their frustrations. It also a great way to acquire inspiration for a book or a painting.

For some reason, keeping journals have not lost its appeal to many young people. Social media is already there for us to indulge in. Apparently, there is a difference between showing off for the sake of validation, and actually recording the most important scenes of your life for personal progress.

We all see how introverts struggle with the fact that they are alone and that they have peculiar qualities that no one else understands. However, if provided with ample time, they will be able to use these very same qualities to their advantage by channeling energies to become more productive and positive, you might as well be closer towards attaining the goals that you set for yourself.

Chapter 16: Non-Verbal Communication

"The typical introvert uses his or her observant nature to read the room. They're more likely to notice people's body language and facial expressions, which makes them better at interpersonal communication."

Dr. Jennifer Kahnweiler

In the last chapter, we learned that messages are conveyed by the words spoken (10%), the tone of voice (40%) and body language (50%).

In this chapter, we will look at the body language aspect of this equation, also referred to as non-verbal communication skills.

As mentioned earlier, as an introvert, you are already adept at reading a room and picking up on non-verbal cues. With just a little more knowledge on what to look for, you truly can be a powerhouse.

Non-Verbal Communication Cues

What do you think the following might mean? If you can think of more than one possibility, write them all down.

Arms crossed

Legs crossed

Knee bouncing

Body turned away

Making eye contact

Not making eye contact

Rolling eyes

Eyes wandering

Eyes closed

Looking toward the door

Looking at the floor

Looking at a watch

Chewing on a pen

Fingers tapping rhythmically

Tapping a single finger

Pointing a finger

Clenched fists

Standing up

Pacing

Slumping in a chair

Leaning back in a chair

Pounding the table

Standing at a distance

Standing very close

Pushing

We will return to the list later, but in the meantime, keep these in mind as you read this chapter.

Gestures

What do you the following gestures mean to you? Are you aware of alternate meanings in other cultures? Are there any you would avoid?

Thumbs up

Palm up and forward

Hand up with fingers spread

Finger and thumb together, forming a circle

Single finger curled towards you, beckoning

Index and baby finger up, middle fingers down

Fist with thumb poking out between the index and second finger

Snapping fingers

We will return to cultural differences later, and these gestures in particular. In the meantime, if more possible meanings come to you, jot them down.

Why Body Language Matters

About 50% of the message one hears is the from the speaker's non-verbal messages. These include eye contact (or lack thereof), arms crossed, chair pushed back, head down, looking away, rolling eyes, rigid back, laid back in the chair, legs crossed (or uncrossed), standing, or sitting.

Some are considered universal (e.g. arms crossed, lack of eye contact), whereas others are particular to the individual (e.g. a person who usually sits stands, or sitting upright when usually laid back).

You have to consider the situation (could the person with their arms crossed simply be cold?) and how well you know the person.

As a general rule, however, these non-verbal cues may not come to you consciously, at least not at first. Your body may react to non-verbal signals before you've even had a chance to think about them.

The same applies to the speaker's tone of voice, which accounts for 40% of the message conveyed. More often than not, your psyche will respond to any tension in the speaker's tone of voice before you have even had a chance to think about it. You may find yourself feeling guarded before you've even heard the essence of the spoken message.

Of course, words are important, but at 10%, you don't want to ignore the power of what you communicate non-verbally at 50%, and the message sent by the tone of your voice, at 40%, as factors in how your entire message comes across.

Body Language for Introverts

Beyond reading the body language of others, there are numerous benefits to monitoring to your own body language.

Paying attention to your body language will help you:

Appear more confident

Feel more confident

Reduce your anxiety

Boost your testosterone

This is especially good news for introverts.

When your anxiety is reduced, your focus will turn outward. And when your attention is directed outside of yourself, you will break the anxiety spiral.

Take a breath and enjoy the experience, as in this improved state you will find yourself having more enriching conversations with others.

Open Body Stance

The key is to adopt an open body stance with an erect posture, standing tall, with your head up, shoulders back and elbows out.

This posture is referred to as 'open' as, in a primitive context, your body is more exposed. In a battle, you would be more vulnerable.

A few hints:

Keep your arms uncrossed. If your arms are crossed, you will begin to feel more anxious. Uncrossing your arms will actually reduce your anxiety.

Plant your feet firmly on the ground, far enough apart to secure your balance. Resist the temptation to balance on one foot or lean against something.

Hold your elbows out from your body. Take up as much room as possible. If you are holding a wine glass, practice holding it away from your body.

Use hand gestures while you are speaking.

When you are talking with someone, nod your head to indicate interest. A 'triple nod' when someone stops speaking will be a signal that you'd like them to continue (try it, it works).

Resist the temptation to check your phone, as you will immediately take on a closed stance, and repel people from you (more on this later in the chapter).

The result of standing with your elbows out and using hand gestures is that your body will physically take up more space. The more space your body takes up, the more confidence you will exude.

You may recognize this posture in speakers and other people with significant personal power. This is what is referred to as a power position, but it doesn't necessarily mean you are seeking power. Rather, you appear confident.

Now let's return to what messages our body language sends to others.

Non-Verbal Communication Cues – A Few Possibilities

Earlier in the chapter, you guessed what a number of non-verbal communication cues might mean. Get out your notes and compare your ideas with the possibilities below.

Arms crossed – might mean:

 Defensive

 Closed to listening

 Cold and trying to warm oneself

Legs crossed – might mean:
 Relaxed
 Defensive
 Physical discomfort
Knee bouncing – might mean:
 Impatience
 Nervous energy
 Excitement
Body turned away crossed – might mean:
 Disinterested
 Closed to ideas
 Desire to flee
Making eye contact – might mean:
 Open
 Challenging (staring)
 Listening
Not making eye contact – might mean:
 Closed
 Avoiding
 Distracted
 Shame
Rolling eyes – might mean:
 Fed up
 Disagreeable

Eyes wandering – might mean:
 Distracted
 Disinterested
 Listening
Eyes closed – might mean:
 Listening
 Thinking
 Concentrating
 Avoidance
 Sleeping
Looking towards the door – might mean:
 Desire to flee
 Distracted
Looking at the floor – might mean:
 Thoughtful
 Distracted
 Shame
Looking at watch – might mean:
 Tight for time
 Distracted
 Desire to leave
Chewing on a pen – might mean:
 Listening
 Thoughtful

Fingers tapping rhythmically — might mean:

 Impatient

 Nervous habit

 Excited

Tapping a single finger – might mean:

 Trying to make a point

 Dominating

 Aggression

Pointing a finger – might mean:

 Accusing

 Authoritarian gesture

 Look there (if pointed away)

Clenched fists – might mean:

 Frustration

 Anger

 Impatience

Standing up – might mean:

 Ready to leave

 Deep in thought

 Physical discomfort

Pacing – might mean:

 Deep in thought

 Worried

Impatience

Slumping in a chair – might mean:

 Relaxed

 Defeated

 Tired

Leaning back in a chair – might mean:

 Relaxed

 Listening

 Disinterested

Pounding the table – might mean:

 Feeling unheard

 Emphasis

 Anger

Standing at a distance – might mean:

 Disengaged

 Respectful

 Aloof

Standing very close – might mean:

 Intimidating

 Disrespectful

 Assertive

Pushing – might mean:

 Assertive

 Disrespectful

Crowd behavior

Cultural Differences

As we have discussed, people from different cultural backgrounds can vary greatly in terms of beliefs, cultural norms and communication styles.

This is perhaps most evident in non-verbal communications.

Eye Contact

In the west, eye contact is not only common; it is expected. If someone does not make eye contact, we think they are hiding something. In other cultures, direct eye contact is seen as rude and confrontational, and avoiding eye contact is a sign of respect.

Personal Space

In the west, we expect a fair amount of personal space around us physically. If someone gets too close, we feel our personal space has been invaded, and we become uncomfortable. If there is incidental touch, we consider the offender to be rude and inconsiderate. Yet, in other cultures, such as highly populated countries, holding back and not asserting yourself physically can be considered a weakness.

Gestures

Gestures have completely different meanings depending upon the part of the world you come from.

If you were traveling, you would probably study the countries and the region you were traveling to in order to learn what gestures are and are not acceptable.

Living in a multicultural society, however, you could unintentionally insult someone you are speaking with by using a gesture that has a completely different meaning in their homeland.

Here are a few examples:

Standing with your hands on your hips conveys confidence and pride and is considered to be a power position in the west, however this stance can be interpreted as challenging or anger.

While winking might mean 'We share a secret,' or a romantic interest in the west, it is considered rude in some cultures. It can also be a signal for children to leave the room.

Slouching may just be seen as lazy or relaxed in the west, but in some cultures, it is a sign of disrespect.

Crossing one's legs, with the bottom of one foot exposed, may be meaningless in the west, but it is considered dirty and rude elsewhere in the world.

Even nodding has different meanings. In the west, nodding your head up and down means yes, and shaking your side-to-side means no, but there are cultures where these meanings are reversed.

Let's return to the list of gestures from earlier in this chapter.

Gestures – Different Cultural Meanings

How many of these were familiar to you? Did you know that any could be considered to be rude or insulting?

Thumbs up – in various cultures, this gesture can mean:
That's ok
Up yours
Palm up and forward – in various cultures, this gesture can mean:
Stop
Settle down
Call a waiter
Hand up with fingers spread – in various cultures, this gesture can mean:
Greeting
Eat shit
Finger and thumb together, forming a circle – in various cultures, this gesture can mean:
OK sign
Your anus
Zero
Single finger curled towards you, beckoning – in various cultures, this gesture can mean:
Come here
Rude, only used for dogs

Death

Index and baby finger up, middle fingers down — in various cultures, this gesture can mean:

Positive

Sign of the devil

Fist with thumb poking out between the index and second finger — in various cultures, this gesture can mean:

Good luck

Fertility

Female genitalia

Screw you

Snapping fingers — in various cultures, this gesture can mean:

I have an idea

Hurry up

Offensive

While you no one can be expected to know what every gesture might mean worldwide, it can only help your interpersonal interactions if you can avoid some common pitfalls.

Context is Everything

Of course, you can't know for sure what is going on with someone without asking them, and that is not always appropriate. So consider the signals you pick up on to be clues, not definitive answers.

On the other hand, if you know the person, you have the extra advantage of knowing what is unusual for them. In a word, you have context. Often it is your knowledge of the person that allows you to become aware of changes in body language that others would miss.

Here are a few scenarios that illustrate this point.

In each situation, what do you think might be going on? Are there any non-verbal cues that a bystander would realize are significant?

A Meeting with Marty

Angelina walked into her boss, Marty's, office. He had a big grin on his face. He was on the phone, so signaled for her to sit, covering the mouthpiece to whisper that he would only be a minute.

Fred's Meeting with Norman

Fred checked his watch and slipped into his boss, Norman's, office. Norman was on the phone, but he signaled for him to sit down. Aside from this, he did not make eye contact.

The Monday Meeting

Melinda worked remotely but called in weekly to a team meeting with her department at home office. Her colleague, Martin, answered, said they were waiting for Maria, and put Melinda on speakerphone. When she heard the project manager, Maria's, voice, apologizing for being late, Melinda put down her pen to listen. Maria cleared her throat and began the meeting. Keith reported on last week's numbers, but then before anyone else could speak Maria said, "Before we get into today's agenda…"

The RRR Rodeo Team Meeting

Ruth, Ralph, Reggie and the rest of the RRR Rodeo team gathered in the Roundup

Meeting Room. When their boss, Rudy, arrived a few minutes late, he didn't say much and shuffled his papers. There were traces of a grin on Rudy's face.

The President Speaks

Nancy slipped into the meeting room late and the President was already speaking. Everyone else was quiet. There were arms crossed and pushed-back chairs.

The Family Business

Jack was part of a business founded by his father, Leo, who now left day-to-day operations to Jack, his brother, Mack, and their sister, Missy. When he got a text to return to the office for a meeting, he didn't think much about it. When he opened the conference room door, Missy, Mack and Mr. Clifton, the family's lawyer, were already seated.

Any guesses? There isn't much to go on, is there? What additional cues might someone familiar with the individuals notice?

In situations where you already know the person (versus meeting a stranger), you have the added advantage of noticing changes in behavior. For example, a co-worker whose expressive eyes you enjoy when they speak is avoiding eye contact. Or a manager who is usually very chatty in welcoming people to meetings today has his head buried in papers as everyone arrives.

Let's return to our scenarios, this time from the perspective of the participants.

In each of these scenarios, there are signals telling the listener something about what was to come. Before a word was spoken, they had a sense of what was going to happen. This time, you have the advantage of this context.

A Meeting with Marty — Angelina's perspective

Angelina walked into her boss, Marty's, office and laughed when she saw the great big grin on his face. He was like a little kid sometimes, she thought. He was on the phone, so signaled for her to sit, covering the mouthpiece to whisper that he would only be a minute. Angelina waited with anticipation, wondering what was up.

Interpretation: Angelina figured good news was coming.

Non-Verbal Cues: the grin on Marty's face, his body language as he signaled for Angelina to sit down.

Fred's Meeting with Norman – Fred's perspective

Fred checked his watch, slipped into his boss, Norman's, office, and took a seat. As usual, Norman was on the phone, but he signaled for him to sit down. Fred immediately felt tense, as he noticed that Norman wasn't making eye contact with him. The two had worked together for years, and Fred instinctively picked up on a change in pattern.

Interpretation: Norman was going to tell Fred something he wasn't going to like.

Non-Verbal Cues: Lack of usual eye contact.

The Monday Meeting – Melinda's perspective

Melinda worked remotely but called in weekly to a team meeting with her department at home office. Her colleague, Martin, picked up the phone when it rang, said "Maria's late, we're just waiting," and put Melinda on speakerphone. It was the usual Monday morning banter, which Melinda half listened to as she made her notes for the meeting. It wasn't quite the same as being there in person, but that was ok; she was used to it. When she heard the project manager, Maria's voice, apologizing for being late, Melina put down her pen to listen. The room was largely quiet as they waited for Maria to start, which she eventually did, by clearing her throat. With a more serious tone than usual, Maria began the meeting. As usual, she had Keith report on last week's numbers, then Maria jumped in before anyone could comment, and said, "Before we get into today's agenda..." Melinda was immediately alert to the seriousness in Maria's voice and held her breath.

Interpretation: Something's up and it's not good news.

Non-Verbal Cues: Maria clearing her throat, the way Maria jumped in before anyone could say anything, Maria's tone of voice.

The RRR Rodeo Team Meeting – Ruth's perspective

Ruth, Ralph, Reggie and the rest of RRR Rodeo team gathered in the Roundup Meeting Room, where they had been beckoned by their boss, Rudy. When Rudy arrived, a few minutes late, he didn't say much (unusual for him) and shuffled his papers, but Ruth could see the traces of a grin playing at the side of his mouth. She wondered what was up.

Interpretation: Ruth suspected good news or some sort of surprise.

Non-Verbal Cues: A change in behavior, and traces of a grin.

The President Speaks – Nancy's perspective

When Nancy slipped into the meeting room late, she couldn't catch the thread of the conversation, but she noticed that the President's tone of voice – usually cheery – was restrained. As she found a seat, she looked around at her colleagues and noticed a lot of crossed arms and pushed-back chairs. Uh oh, she thought, I wonder what's up.

Interpretation: There is bad news afoot, and the others already know it.

Non-Verbal Cues: President's tone of voice, and the body language of her colleagues.

The Family Business – Jack's perspective

Jack was part of a family-run business, founded by his father, Leo. For the most part today, Leo played a behind the scenes role and left day-to-day operations to Jack, his brother, Mack, and their sister, Missy. When he got the text to return to the office for an important meeting, he didn't think much about it. When he opened the conference room door, however, and saw Missy and Mack sitting, with stunned expressions, across from Mr. Clifton, the family's lawyer, he knew it wasn't good news.

Interpretation: Something has happened to dad.

Non-Verbal Cues: The stunned expressions on Missy and Mack's faces, and the presence of Mr. Clifton.

Can you now see the signals that the participants, who were familiar with the players involved, were able to notice?

This doesn't mean that you won't notice non-verbal signals from strangers. You can, but you might not always know for sure what is going on.

It's always wise to withhold judgment, but spend some time observing body language in the meetings you attend and see what you can pick up on.

Message Mismatch

What do you do if you are faced with a disconnect between what someone says and what their body language and/or tone of voice is conveying?

Take a minute to reflect.

If you notice a mismatch between what a person is saying and the other signals you are receiving, your options are either to:

 Do nothing at the moment.

 Ask a question.

 Reflect on the interaction afterward.

 Have a follow-up discussion.

 Still do nothing.

In terms of asking a question, you could ask a specific question about the mismatch or simply mirror back what you observed. Here is some wording that might work:

 "I notice you looking at your watch. Do you have another meeting? Would you like to reschedule for when you have more time?"

 "I'm interested in your feedback on what I have said so far."

"That's what happened, from my perspective. I'd like to hear what happened from your perspective."

"I'm picking up that you may be uncomfortable with what I am saying. Would you like to share what's on your mind?"

"I know you are saying that you are happy with my work on the project, but you are not smiling. Is there something that is concerning you?"

A disconnect between words and non-verbal cues could be a signal that your approach is off, so reflect on the conversation afterward.

For example: If your "Here's how I saw it unfold," brought downcast eyes or crossed arms, perhaps try a different approach next time. For example, "I'd like to share what I observed first, then I'd like to hear what happened from your perspective," may bring a different reaction.

Personal Safety and De-escalating Situations

Sometimes non-verbal cues can tell you that something is seriously off. If someone is acting aggressively–such as yelling, pointing a finger at you–you may need to extricate yourself from the situation for your own safety.

It's also good to know some tricks for de-escalating a situation.

Listening is the most important thing you can do. Ask the other person for their perspective and use your active listening skills until you fully understand things from their angle. Don't disagree or try to solve the problem at this time. Just keep probing until they feel heard. When people feel heard, they are less likely to act with hostility or shut down or refuse to listen.

You might feel like you are the only one steering the boat, but that's ok.

Those Darn Smartphones

Our discussion on non-verbal communication would not be complete without a discussion on the ubiquitous cell phone.

Scrolling or typing on a Smartphone may seem rude to you, but it actually might not be.

In today's culture, many people are so attached to their devices that they can't imagine putting them down. They may believe that they can listen just as well if they are busy on their phone versus not, but not quite. But don't take this alone to be a sign of rudeness.

That said, having your nose stuck in your Smartphone is not going to help your conversation skills. The very act will shut down any possibility of meeting new people, let alone starting new conversations.

Think about what happens when we are engaged with these devices:

What non-verbal signals do you send when you are using your device?

What non-verbal messages have you picked up from others?

If you are somewhere now where people are using their devices, have a look around. What do you notice about their body language?

If you are alone right now, try this exercise when you are next out and about in the world. Look around you and observe the non-verbal messages being sent by those who are busy on their devices.

Next time you go to a meeting or a gathering, observe the other people as they arrive. Who ends up in a conversation first--someone with their head stuck in their phone or the rare person who is waiting patiently for the meeting to begin? Yes, if you'd rather be left alone, then you could consider your phone to be your best friend, but as you have purchased this book on conversation skills, this is probably not your goal. It may be your instinct, but it will not help you interact.

Here's what happens when you are looking at the screen on your Smartphone: Your head is tilted down.

Your shoulders are naturally pulled in.

Your attention is diverted.

Your body language is closed.

The signal you are sending is 'Stay away'.

It is not possible for someone to even catch your eye.

In a word, you are unapproachable.

By the way, any hope you might have that occupying yourself with your phone might suggest that you are very busy, have urgent messages or are otherwise more important than anyone else, is dead. Everyone knows what you are doing because they have done it themselves.

A few final tips about Smartphones:

If you want to meet people, put your phone down. Put it away. Turn it off or put it in silent mode.

When you find yourself alone at an event with no one to talk to, resist the temptation to look at your phone.

If you need to check your phone, step aside and do it, then put it away.

Finally, don't let your phone become a crutch. It's far too easy to cover awkward silences by retreating into your device but resist the temptation. You just might find someone interesting to talk to!

As we wrap up this chapter, here are a few helpful caveats to keep in mind:

As an introvert, you are already adept at picking up on non-verbal cues; keep on learning—you are on your way to becoming a powerhouse.

Keep in mind that a person could have their arms crossed because they are cold, but it could mean something else too.

Reading body language is looking for clues but is not definitive.

Trust your gut. If you get a strong feeling something is amiss, it probably is.

Context is everything. If you know the person and/or the surrounding circumstances, take this into account when interpreting body language.

Consider your own body language.

Body language can mean different things in different cultures.

Voice tone also matters (more on this in Chapter 11).

What do you think? Do you notice other people's non-verbal communications? Since reading this chapter, have you started noticing your own reactions to the non-verbal signals others send out? Do you notice anything you do that sends an unintended message contrary to what you intend?

Case Studies

Rebecca knew she wore her feelings on her sleeve; there was no hiding how she felt! With a greater understanding of non-verbal communication, she was able to be intentional with her body language, so as to not be so overtly emotional in non-critical situations.

Larry was sometimes accused of being defensive, when he didn't think he was. After learning about non-verbal communication, he was able to consciously uncross his arms and make better eye contact. Coupled with his new active listening skills, he stopped hearing this feedback.

Chris didn't understand why everyone thought she was intimidated by others. As she gained an understanding of her body language and the signals she sent out, she was able to make some minor adjustments to appear more confident: not bowing her head, making more eye contact and nodding while listening.

Non-verbal communication was not something Kelly had paid much attention to in the past. Initially, he became fascinated by the non-verbal messages others sent, analyzing people in all sorts of situations. Ultimately, he was able to identify that his habit of throwing down his pen when he was fed up was putting people off. Now he laid his pen down gently.

The Introvert's Survival Guide to Non-Verbal Communication

Your ability to convey open body language and read the non-verbal cues of others can go a long way to improving the effectiveness of your communications.

Here are a few do's and don'ts to keep in mind:

Do's

DO observe the body language of others.

DO be aware of your own body language.

DO use an open body stance (stand tall, shoulders apart).

DO plant your feet firmly on the ground.

DO smile.

DO make eye contact.

DO ask a question.

Don'ts

DON'T cross your arms.

DON'T beat yourself up if you fumble.

DON'T problem-solve if you are angry.

DON'T expect everyone to respond the same.

3 Keys to Remember

KEY 1: Adopt an open body stance.

KEY 2: Stay off your phone.

KEY 3: Communicate that you are approachable.

The Introvert's Survival Guide to Smartphones

Put it away. Just put it away. You don't need your Smartphone to interact with people in person.

Here are a few do's and don'ts to keep in mind:

Do's

DO put your phone away.

DO be the one person in the room who is not on a device.

Don'ts

DON'T hide behind your phone.

DON'T cover awkward pauses by pulling out your phone.

DON'T assume others on their phones are being rude.

3 Keys to Remember

KEY 1: To meet people, put your phone away.

KEY 2: Deal with any urgent matter, then put your device away.

KEY 3: Don't use your phone as a crutch.

Chapter 17: The Introvert In A Relationship

It's surprising just how many relationships are made up of introverts and extroverts, so it is possible to get an introvert involved in a relationship, the trick for a successful relationship is to learn how to balance each other's needs. What are you, are you an introvert, an extrovert or something in between. Some people may be uncomfortable in certain situations but fine in others. If you love an introvert and you are more of an extrovert, it can take time to reconcile your characteristics, but then if you love them, who cares about a bit of time and effort. Introverts tend to be quieter more thoughtful people. They are not always comfortable in busy, crowded situations. Introverts find it easier to recharge their batteries by, maybe reading a good book or by going for a quiet walk. Introverts have a different outlook on life. Introverts tend not to have a wide circle of friends and are more likely to be very loyal to those that they connect with, although, and understandably they expect loyalty in return.

On the other hand, an extrovert tends to be of a livelier disposition who thrives on having a wide circle of friends and in their local social scene. Extroverts can be full on characters which can intimidate introverts, in fact, extroverts can take advantage of an introvert because they are less likely to respond in an overtly negative way, they might not complain but that does not mean that they are happy. They like to live life to the sensory full; they actively seek out excitement and stimuli, whereas an introvert can find stimulation within the mind. In order to get an introvert involved in a relationship, you have to find out what makes them tick, and they likewise have to be able to understand you. The best way to do this is to talk to each other. If an introvert has been alone for too long then they can have problems in communicating their wants and needs, as much as they might want to move forward in life, they might not know how. It could also be the case that their lack of communication with others has made them feel isolated. It can be a long job to draw them out of their shells, but it can be worth it. Don't just talk with your partner; you need to listen to them as well. Your partner needs to have confidence in you that you understand where they are coming from. If there is something that you do not understand then keep asking questions until you do, apart from helping you, it shows that you care. If you hope to get an introvert engaged in a relationship, then at some point you are going to have to tackle the thorny issue of entertainment. You are not going to be able to build a healthy relationship by not going out and sharing some good times together. Start out by going to quite, more intimate places where they can feel comfortable and not overly crowded. If you are used to a livelier social life then your introverted partner cannot expect you to give that up for them, there has to be a compromise as to how you can both move forward together.

One way forward is in how you manage your own lives. If you can strike a balance between doing your own thing and spending time together then you could have a great life together. You have to stay true to who you are or else you lose your identity. There is nothing wrong with the extrovert partner spending time with their friends, just as there is nothing wrong with the introvert being comfortable in their own space. The one thing that you have to be careful of is not to lead lives that are too far apart. Like all couples you have to do things together, you have to share each other's interests, and you have to get to know each other's friends. This might mean that the introvert gets their comfort zone stretched, but then if you don't do things together, are you really a couple?

You can get an introvert engaged in a relationship if you can understand and deal with the intricacies of your marriage. If you are an extrovert and your partner an introvert, you have to understand that neither of you can change who you are, so you have to respect each other for who you are, this means being flexible in your approach to life with each other, and being ready and able to negotiate or compromise when events and schedules clash.

Chapter 18: The Introverted Leader

Leadership is a topic that I'm passionate about. John C. Maxwell, the world's leading leadership guru, defines it, "Leadership is influence. Nothing more, nothing less". Just how important is leadership? Just think about this: behind every great event of achievement, there is a great leader. I strongly believe that as introverts, we have a natural game-field advantage in the realm of leadership.

When I first started learning about leadership, I thought that a leader's ace quality had to be social confidence. This is the reason I used to dislike leadership. I used to think, "How could it be that only those who can talk their way out of any situations can become leaders?" However, as I began learning more and more about the topic, my opinions began to change. First, I learned that eloquent speakers and motivators are not necessarily good leaders. Far from it. "In order to become a leader", I was once told by a mentor, "You will need to develop your character much more than your charisma. Actually, if you had to go on without one of the two, it should be without charisma. Your character will be the foundation of your type of leadership."

My interest towards leadership and so did the time I spent reading about it and connecting it with introversion. Recently, I came across a study that sorted 4591 CEOs of publicly traded US companies and measured their results according to varying levels of introversion and extroversion. They found that CEOs who scored high in extroversion run companies with a 2% less return on assets. The converse is also true: introverted CEOs ran companies that outperformed their peers as a whole.

Why are introverts naturally better at leadership?

Simple. The most important characteristics of leadership are inward qualities. You see, the principles of vision, purpose, and character, among many others on which real leadership is cemented, develop on the inside. Who else better to develop these traits than an introvert that naturally resides in their minds?

Vision and Purpose

I mentioned that behind every great accomplishment, there was a great leader. Let me add that behind every great leader, there's also a very powerful and moving why. Dr. Myles Munroe, a world authority in leadership, and defined leadership as "the capacity to influence others through inspiration motivated by passion, generated by vision, produced by a conviction, ignited by a purpose". The key things here being purpose and vision. Everything begins with a purpose that is maintained and acted upon through the creation of a compelling vision. According to Dr. Myles Munroe, "purpose is when you know and understand what you were born to accomplish. Vision is when you see it in your mind and begin to imagine it". He uses these two concepts as the building blocks of all leadership.

Let's go back to Elon Musk for an example (sorry, being a sci-fi nerd at heart, his life highly intrigues me). Being an outlier from a young age, young Elon spent most of his waking day with his nose stuck in books. It is said that by age 12 or 13, he had read all the books in his local library and had to visit other libraries if he was to continue his incessant pursuit of knowledge. By his teenage years, all of this knowledge that ranged from philosophy to physics pushed him towards an existential crisis. He concluded, "I came to the conclusion that really we should aspire to increase the scope and scale of human consciousness in order to better understand what questions to ask". He elaborated, "The only thing that makes sense to do is strive for greater collective enlightenment." This became his longing.

Over time this desire for collective enlightenment took the shape of something more concrete, but still seemingly absurd- a personal life purpose dedicated saving humanity from extinction and turning humans into space colonizers. Yes, you read that correctly. This shy kid from South Africa sought to find purpose in his life and he found it. The years that followed are only proof of this. From leaving a comfortable life in South Africa and emigrating to Canada and eventually the USA, to building a rocket factory in the middle of Los Angeles- he has done it all in pursuit of this purpose. The businesses he has created and the staggering 20 billion dollar net worth he has built for himself have never been the end he sought. They were nothing but stepping stones for what he needed to accomplish. Musks stated in an interview, "I would like to die thinking that humanity has a bright future. If we can solve sustainable energy and be well on our way to becoming a multi-planetary species with a self-sustaining civilization on another planet- to cope with a worst-case scenario happening and extinguishing human consciousness- then, I think that would be a good thing."

One might easily conclude that the idea that one could plan out his life to that detail is absurd. Well, Musk would think otherwise. He states, "It is not [his success story] some story invented after the fact. I don't want to seem like a Johnny-come-lately or that I'm chasing a fad or just being opportunistic. I'm not an investor. I like to make technologies real that I think are important for the future and useful in some sort of way".

When faced to question as to what his ultimate vision is, we need not even ask. If one were to visit the SpaceX HQ near the Los Angeles International Airport, one can see his ultimate vision. On the way to Musk's cubicle, you will find two posters on an adjacent wall. The poster on the left depicts Mars as it is today: a red, pale, cold, lifeless planet. On the right, you will find Mars terraformed into a suitable place for human life. It is filled with green all around and projects warmth. That's Elon's ultimate goal.

Picture of SpaceX Headquarters. Taken from

Doesn't the idea of saving humanity excite you as a human being? Doesn't the vision of terraforming a planet motivate you? Imagine what it does for Elon who's the one actually living it. Do you think that Elon ever gets bored? Perhaps during mundane waits or when dealing trivial matters. However, his life and the way he lives according to his sense of purpose and vision grant him unbounded energy to continue his pursuit. All of his accomplishments prove this point. This is the secret behind every great leader.

What does this all have to do with introversion? The development of a vision and purpose is a process that occurs within. To find purpose in your life, you have to start with yourself by evaluating your feelings about the status quo. Do you feel passionate towards a specific topic? Do you find yourself daydreaming about doing something in particular? Is there anything in your life that the mere thought of excites you and fills you with energy? It is through asking these questions and sincerely evaluating their answers that one gets a notion of what he or she was born to do in their lifetime. We all have unique talents, unique desires, and unique motives; and we have all felt at one point a longing to use them to do great things. I invite you to make a journey within, a journey of recollection. Freely explore all the potential you've inhibited in the past. While it might be hard to pinpoint exactly, as an introvert it will be easier to find your purpose.

After finding a motive or purpose, choose to project inside of your mind an image of the ideal you're in pursuit of. This image will become your vision, your definite goal or aim. Your purpose will never change completely, but your vision will progressively evolve as you accomplish the aims you've placed before yourself. Can you remember how, as a kid, you'd wander off for hours inside your head? Living in fantasy worlds and being in bliss? This is exactly what I am inviting you to do-something we're already great at. Create a powerful mental image of what is desired and to replay this image constantly in your mind until it becomes something you naturally work towards for. This is the cure for procrastination, boredom, and other modern-day 'ailments'.

Conscious Decision Making and Taking Action

It is thought that introverts are slower to take action than extroverts. Extroverts are known for making fast decisions and getting things done, while introverts usually wonder and ponder. I want to challenge this assumption because, to me, it couldn't be further from the truth. One thing is to take action for the sake of taking action. Another thing is taking conscious meaningful action. Let me explain.

I once asked a close mentor of mines why it was that I wasn't making improvements in my life. I dreamt out a life with rich relationships, economic abundance, and lasting fulfillment. I was far from it. He responded with the following metaphor:

This is the story of Jane and John. Jane was by far the prettiest girl in town and the envy of all her female peers. Tall, blonde, and fine, she had a charming sass that drew in all the men that crossed her path. Her charm was not only in the physical but also in the intellectual. She was working for a prestigious firm and made enough money to live comfortably. Yet, despite all of this, you wouldn't believe who she decided to have as a boyfriend. His name was John and he was the antithesis of Jane. Ugly, crude and untactful, He was a lazy alcoholic who would spend his days at home, living on Jane's money. Jane's girlfriends encouraged her to dump him. She wouldn't budge. She was deeply in love.

One day as she drove to work, she noticed the entire building was closed. Everyone had taken the day off for an important event. What a lucky day! Jane decided then that the rest of the day would be spent with John. Her plan consisted of going to do groceries, cooking something together at home and later on the night go out to the movies. It was the perfect day. After a couple of hours of grocery shopping, she went back home. She opened to front door and her ears met a wonderful music coming from her room. "John must be in a good mood. He's not one to put up music throughout the day". She walked down the hall to greet him. She opened her room only to find him in bed with another woman. Tears rushed down her face as she began to frantically kick the woman out of her bed and her house. Words couldn't begin to describe her anger and disappointment. She told John to leave the house for good. She wouldn't ever see him again.

The next few days were a living hell for Jane. Depression overcame her and her friends could do nothing about it. They began to worry. The following week something great occurred. Her best friend visited after work and left her a gift. "Look I know you've been going through a lot. I recently won this trip on a cruise all-inclusive. I was going to go, but I'd rather have you go instead. You need to start living again."

Jane looked up. "But how will a going on a cruise make me start living again?"

"It's not just a cruise. You're the only female who will go. In it, there will be hundreds of men all looking to court you. Guess what? They're all hot and ready to find the love of their life. It could be you!"

Jane yielded. And as she did, she began getting excited. Perhaps not all was bad. Perhaps she could finally find Mr. Right.

The day to board the cruise finally arrived and she couldn't be more excited. She received VIP service in every aspect of her stay. As she boarded the ship, she was led to her Diamond Suite, and upon entering was presented with the most beautiful collection of dresses she had ever seen in her life. "Go ahead and choose the dress that you like. And after you're done, call me so we can get your hair done", said the butler. She was ecstatic. "Remember, after we're done, we'll go to the main banquet area where the men are waiting for you. Let's start!"

After a few hours of preparation, she was finally ready. She turned to the mirror and couldn't believe the figure facing her was really... her. "I truly am beautiful".

She walked down from her room and into the banquet area and encountered the most enticing and beautiful men of her life. She proceeded to chat them up one by one throughout the night. It was amazing and she was having a blast. Among the multitude of handsome men, one of them stood out. His name was Peter. He was tall, handsome and had this peculiar trait about him that made him irresistible for Jane. She couldn't pinpoint what it was, but she really liked him!

They started dating after the cruise and formed a serious relationship. After a few months, they chose to move in together. Everything was great until... she actually got to know him. Little by little qualities of laziness and rudeness began to flower and she eventually saw Peter for who he was-an exact replica of John!

"Gerald, you see, just like Jane, people repeat patterns. We live in circles or cycles in which we repeat things subconsciously as to get the result we're programmed to get. The human mind may be infinitely powerful; however, it is very lazy and despises change. Change means work and our brain is all about preserving energy and working as little as possible." What a horrible thing! This is why people, unless they take the time to do some introspection, will always end up repeating the same cycle in their life.

Carl Jung once said, "Until you make the subconscious conscious, it will direct your life and you will call it fate". To begin a process of change and take meaningful action, we must sit and ponder. We must analyze the actions we take repeatedly and the results they've generated. This is what conscious decision making is all about; gauging your next action according to your thoughts, intuition, and definite aim. And, as you might've guessed, it's an activity that thrives on introversion.

So, to those that argue that extroverts are faster at making decisions and taking action, I would say, "Depends on what kind of action we're talking about." It is very easy to continue repeating a self-degenerating cycle. It is easy to work very hard and consistently, yet if you are to waste most of your money in mundane activities that don't get you where you want, then are you really taking action towards an ideal? Or are you just being subject to your subconscious mind?

Exuding Calmness

"Being calm in tough situations is a super power."

- Unknown

I believe that one of the true marks of a great leader is staying grounded in moments of panic. A stronger will is not shown through reactivity. It is through pro-activity that we find solutions to problems. The loud, shifting action taker will oversee details, and is more likely to cause problems than the individual who is willing to sit down and see the bigger picture.

In the alpha-obsessed culture that we live in, we dismiss the strength found in tranquility. Therefore, it's hard to see that reactivity is actually a beta trait. Reactivity (or lack of conscious decision making manifested in e.g. shouting and getting angry) to tough situations is a sign of instability or fear. It springs out of the need to look good and defend one's own self-image. To illustrate, take a manager afraid of missing a deadline. Getting angry, blaming others and putting them down for their lack of participation will not improve the situation- rather it will do the complete opposite. A leader or a true 'alpha' is someone solves problems and give their people confidence that everything will be alright. It's the person that, when problems arise, will sit down, talk and negotiate with team members and think out solutions. He or she will choose the best solution for the team (even if it's at their own expense) and have everyone act upon it.

Think of reactivity as when something breaks due to pressure applied to it, such as a pencil. It looks sturdy, but given enough pressure, it will break. Pro-activity is more like a palm tree. A palm tree may be whipped by the wind, but it will always bounce come back to its original position. The latter is where true strength resides.

Thoroughness

"It's not that I'm so smart, it's that I stay with problems longer."

- Albert Einstein

Perhaps it's the stimuli that we get from the outside, or perhaps it's the saturated minds we carry, but whenever introverts encounter a problem, they are thorough in solving it. And this is a great quality to have. The majority of what looks like small problems may have deeper roots that can be easily overlooked. It's like the metaphor of the tip of the iceberg. The tip of the iceberg, or the visible problem, accounts for only 5% of what's truly going on. The remaining 95% remains a mystery to most.

I remember clearly an instance where I was working with a team of people in trying to reach a goal in sales. We tried as much as we could; however, the goal was not being met. I reflected on what could be going wrong. The goal was very clear, people know what to do, and they had an incentive. I was recommended by superiors to demand more out of my people, but I knew that wasn't the case. It was something more personal; I knew that the energy around the team was off. I personally sat down 1 on 1 with everyone in the team. Then I found something. It was during a conversation Kathy, one of my team leaders.

"What do you mean, Kat?"

"Well, I feel out of place telling you this but I've heard Ralph might be leaving the team for good. I'm not sure though, so don't take my word for it", she answered.

After delving into further, I soon learned that there were negative rumors going around about me that originated from somebody's upcoming departure. It would've been natural to react with anger and confront the culprit. However, I decided to sit and ponder. What did I do to get someone to defame me?

I reached out to the culprit. He denied all the accusations of defamation but confirmed that he was soon leaving the organization. I decided to apologize to him.

"Look, Ralph, I'm very sorry if I offended you. Please know that my intention was always to add value to those around me. It's alright if you won't tell me what happened, but I hope we can remain friends no matter what occurs from this point on."

Ralph was never clear on exactly what I did wrong. He soon left afterward and some people left alongside with him. My next step was to apologize to the entire team and be more open to their feedback on the way the organization operated. Through this, I was able to salvage the relationship with the rest of the team. It took us a bit longer to reach our goal, but it was reached nonetheless and our standard for work took a giant leap forward.

I mention this as an example of thoroughness. We introverts process things further, and usually take things deeper. This might cause a delay in some situations but can also be the panacea for many. Had I pushed on the idea of more production like my superiors suggested, the team and our productivity would've suffered tremendously. Sometimes it is infinitely better to sit in stillness and use our thoughts and intuition to detect our next move.

Listening

"The ear of the leader must ring with the voices of the people"

- Woodrow Wilson

Because listening is such a crucial part of building a relationship, it is also a given that it'd be a requirement for good leadership. A great leader knows that the best way to get someone to do something is to get them to want to do it. Well, how do you go about doing that? Simple. Make them your friend. When you've shown empathy to a staff member and connected with them, they're more willing to do things for you because they like you.

Listening is also the foundation for decision making in leadership positions. In order to make conscious decisions surrounding an organization and take the corresponding action, you have to be well informed. Only a leader who listens to their people will understand what's truly going on. Try imagining a table full of executives and try to pinpoint the leader. Is it the one talking all the time? Or is it the one eliciting the others for the information required to make a good decision?

Introversion and the Law of Legacy

One of the best reasons introverts make great leaders is our dislike for being the center of attention. When you're not the center of attention, your sense of ego doesn't get in the way of being of service to others. More importantly, it allows others to shine and continue our legacy.

Let me elaborate. First, leadership is about service. Take any great leader in history and you will see a perfect example of a life dedicated to service. Jesus, Gandhi, and Mother Theresa are some of these examples. They are people that devoted their lives to work, not for themselves- but for the benefit of others. Because of their genuine service to others, people followed them. Some even gave up their lives for them. Can you see then how the need for being recognized and having themselves as the center of attention could've gotten in the way of their mission?

When I started out in leadership I was a mess (I still am one now, just not as bad). I thought leaders had to be the center of attention, and I did everything to stand out. I soon learned that people will never follow a leader with self-indulgent behavior out of their own will. The people that work for you expect you to care and look out for them. That's why they see you as a leader. The moment they get the idea that they're being used to the leader's personal benefit, the trust built between them disappears, along with your influence over them. My need to look good made my team uneasy around me and most wound up leaving.

Second, until we're able to put the spotlight on somebody else, we cannot fulfill the largest task placed in front of a leader: the creation of a legacy. In his book, The 21 Laws of Leadership, John C. Maxwell dedicates a chapter to his final law: the Law of Legacy. According to him, "A leader's lasting value is measured by succession." Legacy is leaving something behind after a leader has stepped down from his/her position or passed on. In essence, it's about putting the spotlight on somebody else who will carry the organization's vision, purpose, and values. A person too attached to being the center of attention will never be capable of doing this.

The greatest example I can think of is that of Jesus, perhaps the greatest leader in human history thus far. He lived an exemplary life devoted to service and passed on his legacy to only 12 individuals within a 3 year period. After his death at the age of 33, these 12 individuals were instructed to share that which they witnessed with their mentor to anyone who may listen. It's been over 2000 years since his death, and the man lives on through the pope, the church and loyal followers around the planet. I'm not a Christian nor am I advocating a particular religion. However, in terms of leadership, Jesus' lasting legacy is perhaps one of the largest accomplishments ever witnessed.

What are we if not the ideas that our lives come to represent? A person willing to step down and let somebody else shine has the opportunity of having their ideas live on through them.

I want to end this chapter with a quote from the Canadian astronaut Chris Hadfield:

"Ultimately, leadership is not about glorious crowning acts. It's about keeping your team focused on a goal and motivated to their best to achieve it, especially when the stakes are high and the consequences really matter. It is about laying the groundwork for others' success, and then standing back and letting them shine".

Conclusion

People are curious; they want to know something about people around them in order to feel safe, to know how to respond and what to say and do - or not say or do. In short, they need to know, like and trust you (essential for business), but in order to do that they need to flesh out that vague outline of you that you may be presenting to them. If they have no idea who you are, what you stand for, and what delights you or not, they will make something up. In fact, they will write a whole life story for you that would astound you if you knew it. And you probably won't like it.

But I also know that you risk being thought of as "aloof," "snobbish," or even "arrogant." So take a deep breath and learn to say something like, "I had a great time relaxing, getting caught up, and even finding time to read. How about you?" Over to the other person, who probably really wanted to talk about what he or she did, anyway. Use your great listening skills to convince people that you are a great conversationalist.